Theology and Ethics

God *the* Holy Spirit

The Person of the Holy Spirit

. . . .

The Prophetic Work of the Holy Spirit

. . . .

The Powerful Presence of the Holy Spirit I

. . . .

The Powerful Presence of the Holy Spirit II

This curriculum is the result of thousands of hours of work by The Urban Ministry Institute (TUMI) and should not be reproduced without their express permission. TUMI supports all who wish to use these materials for the advance of God's Kingdom, and affordable licensing to reproduce them is available. Please confirm with your instructor that this book is properly licensed. For more information on TUMI and our licensing program, visit *www.tumi.org* and *www.tumi.org/license*.

Capstone Module 14: God the Holy Spirit Student Workbook

ISBN: 978-1-62932-014-4

Contents

1

2

3

4

About the Instructor

Terry Cornett (B.S., M. A., M.A.R.) is Academic Dean Emeritus of The Urban Ministry Institute in Wichita, Kansas. He holds degrees from The University of Texas at Austin, the Wheaton College Graduate School, and the C. P. Haggard School of Theology at Azusa Pacific University.

Terry ministered for 23 years as an urban missionary with World Impact before his retirement in 2005. During that time he served in Omaha, Los Angeles, and Wichita where he was involved in church-planting, education, and leadership-training ministries.

Introduction to the Module

Greetings, in the name of the Father, the Son, and the Holy Spirit!

There are few theological truths in the history of the Church that have sparked as much controversy, disagreement, and schism as the doctrine of the Holy Spirit. From ancient disagreements about Trinity and "procession" to modern disagreements about the baptism and gifts of the Holy Spirit, there is much that might cause us to approach this module with caution; but, I sincerely hope that this is not the case. The doctrine of the Holy Spirit lies at the very heart of the way that we understand who God is and how we experience his living presence in our midst. The Spirit is sent to empower and lead the Church of God and to give new life to all those who respond in faith to its message about Jesus. Our hope is that the truths you learn about the Holy Spirit will not only be "formal theology" which helps you *to understand* God better, but will be also "practical theology" which allows you *to depend on the Holy Spirit* in ever increasing measure as you minister in God's Church and witness in the world.

The first lesson, *The Person of the Holy Spirit*, focuses upon God the Spirit as the third person of the one Trinitarian God. We will explore the biblical portrayal of the Spirit as a divine person who both *is* God and who *consciously acts* as God. We will also discuss the relationship of the Spirit to the Father and the Son as the one who is the "bond of love" between them and their "gift of love to the world." We will talk about the Spirit as the "Life-giver" and show how the names, titles, and symbols of the Spirit in the Scriptures portray him as the source and sustainer of physical and spiritual life and as the one who is at work to renew all things.

In our second lesson, *The Prophetic Work of the Holy Spirit*, we will explore the nature of prophetic revelation and come to understand the Spirit as the one who both *inspires* and *illuminates* the Word of God. We will also see that the prophetic role of the Spirit includes his ministry of conviction. He is the one who overcomes the deception caused by sin and leads us to true repentance. The prophetic work of the Holy Spirit is both the means by which God reveals himself and the means by which he enables us to believe that revelation.

Lessons three and four deal with *The Powerful Presence of the Holy Spirit (Part One)* and *The Powerful Presence of the Holy Spirit (Part Two)*, respectively. Here the focus is on what the Holy Spirit does in the lives of those who repent and believe. We will speak about the role of the Spirit in regeneration, adoption, baptism, gifting, indwelling, sealing, and sanctification. We will come to understand that the powerful work of the Spirit enables the Church to fulfill its mission in the world.

The person of the Holy Spirit is as real and vital as God the Father and God the Son. The Spirit is sent by the Father and the Son into the world so that we can experience loving fellowship with them and so that we can be empowered to obey God's commands and accomplish his mission. Our prayer is that your dependance on the Spirit will grow as you study the Scriptures together.

- Rev. Terry G. Cornett

Course Requirements

Required Books and Materials

- Bible (for the purposes of this course, your Bible should be a translation [ex. NIV, NASB, RSV, KJV, NKJV, etc.], and not a paraphrase [ex. The Living Bible, The Message]).

- Each Capstone module has assigned textbooks which are read and discussed throughout the course. We encourage you to read, reflect upon, and respond to these with your professors, mentors, and fellow learners. Because of the fluid availability of the texts (e.g., books going out of print), we maintain our *official* Capstone Required Textbook list on our website. Please visit *www.tumi.org/books* to obtain the current listing of this module's texts.

- Paper and pen for taking notes and completing in-class assignments.

Suggested Readings

- Fee, Gordon D. *Paul, the Spirit, and the People of God*. Peabody, MA: Hendrickson, 1996.

Suggested Resource

- *The Trinity Pamphlet*. Torrance, CA: Rose Publishing, Inc., 2005 (www.rose-publishing.com).

Summary of Grade Categories and Weights

Attendance & Class Participation. . . . .   30%   90 pts

Quizzes . . . .   10%   30 pts

Memory Verses . . . .   15%   45 pts

Exegetical Project . . . .   15%   45 pts

Ministry Project. . . . .   10%   30 pts

Readings and Homework Assignments. . . . .   10%   30 pts

Final Exam . . . .   <u>10%   30 pts</u>

Total: 100%   300 pts

Grade Requirements

Attendance at each class session is a course requirement. Absences will affect your grade. If an absence cannot be avoided, please let the Mentor know in advance. If you miss a class it is your responsibility to find out the assignments you missed, and to talk with the Mentor about turning in late work. Much of the learning associated with this course takes place through discussion. Therefore, your active involvement will be sought and expected in every class session.

Every class will begin with a short quiz over the basic ideas from the last lesson. The best way to prepare for the quiz is to review the Student Workbook material and class notes taken during the last lesson.

The memorized Word is a central priority for your life and ministry as a believer and leader in the Church of Jesus Christ. There are relatively few verses, but they are significant in their content. Each class session you will be expected to recite (orally or in writing) the assigned verses to your Mentor.

The Scriptures are God's potent instrument to equip the man or woman of God for every work of ministry he calls them to (2 Tim. 3.16-17). In order to complete the requirements for this course you must do an inductive Bible study (i.e., an exegetical study) on Romans 8.1-27. The study will have to be five pages in length (double-spaced, typed or neatly hand written) and should explain what can be learned from this passage about the work of the Holy Spirit. Our desire and hope is that you will be deeply convinced of Scripture's ability to change and practically affect your life, and the lives of those to whom you minister. The details of the project are covered on pages 10-11, and will be discussed in the introductory session of this course.

Ministry Project

Our expectation is that all students will apply their learning practically in their lives and in their ministry responsibilities. The student will be responsible for developing a ministry project that combines principles learned with practical ministry. The details of this project are covered on page 12, and will be discussed in the introductory session of the course.

Class and Homework Assignments

Classwork and homework of various types may be given during class by your Mentor or be written in your Student Workbook. If you have any question about what is required by these or when they are due, please ask your Mentor.

Readings

It is important that the student read the assigned readings from the text and from the Scriptures in order to be prepared for class discussion. Please turn in the "Reading Completion Sheet" from your Student Workbook on a weekly basis. There will be an option to receive extra credit for extended readings.

Take-Home Final Exam

At the end of the course, your Mentor will give you a final exam (closed book) to be completed at home. You will be asked a question that helps you reflect on what you have learned in the course and how it affects the way you think about or practice ministry. Your Mentor will give you due dates and other information when the Final Exam is handed out.

Grading

The following grades will be given in this class at the end of the session, and placed on each student's record:

A - Superior work	D - Passing work
B - Excellent work	F - Unsatisfactory work
C - Satisfactory work	I - Incomplete

Letter grades with appropriate pluses and minuses will be given for each final grade, and grade points for your grade will be factored into your overall grade point average. Unexcused late work or failure to turn in assignments will affect your grade, so please plan ahead, and communicate conflicts with your instructor.

Exegetical Project

As a part of your participation in the Capstone God the Holy Spirit module of study, you will be required to do an exegesis (inductive study) of one of the following passages concerning the work of the Holy Spirit:

- ☐ John 14.15-18
- ☐ Romans 8.1-27
- ☐ 1 Corinthians 2.9-16
- ☐ John 16.7-11
- ☐ Romans 8.12-17
- ☐ Galatians 4.4-7

The purpose of this project is to give you an opportunity to do a detailed study of a major passage on the work of the Holy Spirit. Using the text as a foundation, think critically about the ways in which these Scriptures make plain the role of the Holy Spirit in the life of the believer, the Church, and the world. As you study the text, our hope is that your analysis will deepen your understanding of the way that the Holy Spirit works to accomplish God's mission in the world. We also desire that the Spirit will give you insight as to how you can relate its meaning directly to your own personal walk of discipleship, as well as to the leadership role God has given to you in your church and ministry.

This is a Bible study project, and, in order to do *exegesis*, you must be committed to understand the meaning of the passage in its own setting. Once you know what it meant, you can then draw out principles that apply to all of us, and then relate those principles to life. A simple three step process can guide you in your personal study of the Bible passage:

1. What was *God saying to the people in the text's original situation*?

2. What principle(s) does *the text teach that is true for all people everywhere*, including today?

3. What is *the Holy Spirit asking me to do with this principle here, today*, in my life and ministry?

Once you have answered these questions in your personal study, you are then ready to write out your insights for your *paper assignment*.

Here is a *sample outline* for your paper:

1. List out what you believe is *the main theme or idea* of the text you selected.

2. *Summarize the meaning* of the passage (you may do this in two or three paragraphs, or, if you prefer, by writing a short verse-by-verse commentary on the passage).

3. *Outline one to three key principles or insights* this text provides on the work of the Holy Spirit and the way Christians should respond to him.

4. Tell how one, some, or all of the principles may relate to *one or more* of the following:

   a. Your personal spirituality and walk with Christ

   b. Your life and ministry in your local church

   c. Situations or challenges in your community and general society

As an aid or guide, please feel free to read the course texts and/or commentaries, and integrate insights from them into your work. Make sure that you give credit to whom credit is due if you borrow or build upon someone else's insights. Use in-the-text references, footnotes, or endnotes. Any way you choose to cite your references will be acceptable, as long as you 1) use only one way consistently throughout your paper, and 2) indicate where you are using someone else's ideas, and are giving them credit for it. (For more information, see *Documenting Your Work: A Guide to Help You Give Credit Where Credit Is Due* in the Appendix.)

Make certain that your exegetical project, when turned in meets the following standards:

- It is legibly written or typed.

- It is a study of one of the passages above.

- It is turned in on time (not late).

- It is 5 pages in length.

- It follows the outline given above, clearly laid out for the reader to follow.

- It shows how the passage relates to life and ministry today.

Do not let these instructions intimidate you; this is a Bible study project! All you need to show in this paper is that you *studied* the passage, *summarized* its meaning, *drew out* a few key principles from it, and *related* them to your own life and ministry.

Grading

The exegetical project is worth 45 points, and represents 15% of your overall grade, so make certain that you make your project an excellent and informative study of the Word.

Ministry Project

The Word of God is living and active, and penetrates to the very heart of our lives and innermost thoughts (Heb. 4.12). James the Apostle emphasizes the need to be doers of the Word of God, not hearers only, deceiving ourselves. We are exhorted to apply the Word, to obey it. Neglecting this discipline, he suggests, is analogous to a person viewing our natural face in a mirror and then forgetting who we are, and are meant to be. In every case, the doer of the Word of God will be blessed in what he or she does (James 1.22-25).

Our sincere desire is that you will apply your learning practically, correlating your learning with real experiences and needs in your personal life, and in your ministry in and through your church. Therefore, a key part of completing this module will be for you to design a ministry project to help you share some of the insights you have learned from this course with others.

There are many ways that you can fulfill this requirement of your study. You may choose to conduct a brief study of your insights with an individual, or a Sunday School class, youth or adult group or Bible study, or even at some ministry opportunity. What you must do is discuss some of the insights you have learned from class with your audience. (Of course, you may choose to share insights from your Exegetical Project in this module with them.)

Feel free to be flexible in your project. Make it creative and open-ended. At the beginning of the course, you should decide on a context in which you will share your insights, and share that with your instructor. Plan ahead and avoid the last minute rush in selecting and carrying out your project.

After you have carried out your plan, write and turn in to your Mentor a one-page summary or evaluation of your time of sharing. A sample outline of your Ministry Project summary is as follows:

1. Your name

2. The place where you shared, and the audience with whom you shared

3. A brief summary of how your time went, how you felt, and how they responded

4. What you learned from the time

The Ministry Project is worth 30 points and represents 10% of your overall grade, so make certain to share your insights with confidence and make your summary clear.

LESSON 1

The Person of the Holy Spirit

Lesson Objectives

Welcome in the strong name of Jesus Christ! After your reading, study, discussion, and application of the materials in this lesson, you will be able to:

- Describe the essential Christian understanding of God as Trinity.

- Use the Scriptures to defend the truth that the Holy Spirit is fully God.

- Use the Scriptures to defend the truth that the Holy Spirit is a Divine Person.

- Explain the *filioque* and briefly describe the theological disagreements which have resulted from it.

- Understand and defend the theological reasons for believing that the Spirit proceeds from the Father and the Son.

- Explain Augustine's definition of the Holy Spirit as the "bond of love" between the Father and the Son.

- Explain why the Holy Spirit must be worshiped and glorified along with the Father and the Son.

- Understand why the theological study of the Holy Spirit is called *Pneumatology*.

- Summarize the Old Testament view of the Spirit of God.

- Use the Scriptures to describe the life-giving role of the Spirit in creating and sustaining the world.

- Identify the major symbols associated with the Holy Spirit in the Scriptures and show how they contribute to our understanding of him as the Life-giver.

- Explain how the names and titles of the Holy Spirit in the Scriptures contribute to our understanding of him as the Life-giver.

- Explain why the ministry of the Spirit is a source of hope.

The Spirit Who Makes God Known

Devotion

Read 1 Corinthians 2.10-11 and Romans 8.26. The Spirit of God is remarkable. On the one hand, he explores the deepest mysteries of the Father's mind and will. He possesses infinite knowledge and understanding. And yet, on the other hand, it is the Spirit's special ministry to be near to us, to help us understand who God is and what he desires. The Holy Spirit is, in the teaching of 1 Corinthians 2, the one who reveals God's hidden wisdom and mysteries to us. And, as the reading from Romans points out, the Spirit will pray the will of God in and through us when our human understanding has reached its limits and we do not know what or how we should pray. As we begin our study of the theology of the Holy Spirit, we are faced with the great irony that we cannot understand the Spirit of God without having the help of the Spirit of God. If we truly grasp this truth it should produce both humility and gratitude. We are humbled because we realize that we cannot know God through their own efforts (no matter how hard we study), but only through the work of the Spirit. We are grateful because we know that Spirit is given to us through the sure promises of God and that he is already at work on our behalf to lead us into all truth.

After reciting and/or singing the Nicene Creed (located in the Appendix), pray the following prayer:

Nicene Creed and Prayer

> *O gracious and holy Father, give us wisdom to perceive you, intelligence to understand you, diligence to seek you, patience to wait for you, eyes to behold you, a heart to meditate on you, and a life to proclaim you through the power of the Spirit of Jesus Christ our Lord. Amen.*

> ~ St. Benedict.
> From William Lane, S. J. **Praying with the Saints**. Dublin, Ireland: Veritas, 1989. p. 26.

No quiz this lesson

Quiz

No Scripture memorization this lesson

Scripture Memorization Review

No assignments due this lesson

Assignments Due

CONTACT

Picture Book Theology

1 Draw a simple picture that represents the Holy Spirit. After you have finished, be prepared to explain your drawing to others.

Contending for the Faith

2 The Church in every age has encountered "false teachers" who twist the Scriptures, using them to teach ideas completely contrary to that of Jesus and his Apostles. These false doctrines (heresies) seem to get "recycled," so that the same mistaken ideas find new advocates in each generation. One wrong idea about the Holy Spirit that shows up repeatedly is the belief that the Spirit is some sort of spiritual energy (or spiritual consciousness) but not a Divine Person who speaks and acts as the Living God. (In our day, groups like the *Jehovah's Witnesses* or *The Unity School of Christianity* would teach this false view.) Most popular Christian teaching today focuses on the work of the Holy Spirit; what he *does* in the lives of believers. Can you think of any reason why it might be equally important to teach about who the Holy Spirit *is*?

Three-In-One

3 What do we mean when we say that God is a Trinity? What illustrations have you heard used to try and describe the Trinity? What are the strengths and weaknesses of each illustration?

The Person of the Holy Spirit

Segment 1

Rev. Terry G. Cornett

Summary of
Segment 1

In this first segment, we will focus on the Holy Spirit as Lord, the one who like the Father and the Son, is a full and co-equal member of the Holy Trinity. We will attempt to understand the relationship he has to the Father and the Son and the ways in which the Church has tried to explain this difficult doctrine. Finally, we will emphasize the need to worship God as Trinity, giving glory to the Father and the Son and the Holy Spirit equally and indivisibly.

Our objective for this first segment of *The Person of the Holy Spirit* is to enable you to:

- Describe the essential Christian understanding of God as Trinity.

- Use the Scriptures to defend the truth that the Holy Spirit is fully God.

- Use the Scriptures to defend the truth that the Holy Spirit is a Divine Person.

- Explain the *filioque* and briefly describe the theological disagreements which have resulted from it.

- Understand and defend the theological reasons for believing that the Spirit proceeds from the Father and the Son.

- Explain Augustine's definition of the Holy Spirit as the "bond of love" between the Father and the Son.

- Explain why the Holy Spirit must be worshiped and glorified along with the Father and the Son.

I. Introduction

A. The Nicene Creed

1. See Appendix 1 for a copy of the Nicene Creed.

2. Why use the Nicene Creed?

3. The Bible is the only infallible source of doctrine for the Church. The Nicene Creed is not authoritative in and of itself but only because it carefully summarizes what the Bible teaches.

4. "Those ancient Councils of Nicea, Constantinople, the first of Ephesus, Chalcedon, and the like, which were held for refuting errors, we willingly embrace, and reverence as sacred, in so far as relates to doctrines of faith, for they contain nothing but the pure and genuine interpretation of Scripture" (John Calvin, *Institutes*, IV, ix.8).

B. The doctrine of the Trinity

Tri-Unity [trinity] is a shorthand term used to express in a single word what Scripture teaches in many discrete passages but which took the proclaiming church some time to think through and organize in a clear and distinct teaching . . .
~ Thomas C. Oden

1. The Trinity is the term used by the Church to describe how God is one God, eternally existing in three Persons.

2. The Scriptures assert that God is one, and that there is none other than the one God, and yet they also assert that this one God reveals himself as God the Father, God the Son, and God the Holy Spirit.

3. Trinitarian theology affirms that the members of the Trinity, are in fact one, diverse, and equal, together comprising the one true and undivided God, who eternally exists as Father, Son, and Holy Spirit or as the Athanasian Creed says: *The Father is almighty, the Son is almighty, the Holy Spirit is almighty. Yet there are not three almighty beings; there is but one Almighty Being.*

C. This Trinitarian God is the one we encounter in Scripture through:

1. Threefold Address

    a. Isa. 6.3 - And one called to another and said: "*Holy, holy, holy* is the Lord of hosts; the whole earth is full of his glory!" [Note also v. 8 where God says, "Whom shall I send and who will go for us?"]

    b. Rev. 4.8 - And the four living creatures, each of them with six wings, are full of eyes all around and within, and day and night they never cease to say, "*Holy, holy, holy,* is the Lord God Almighty, who was and is and is to come!"

2. Threefold Appearances

    a. Gen. 18.2-3,10 - He lifted up his eyes and looked, and behold, *three men* were standing in front of him. When he saw *them,* he ran from the tent door to meet them and bowed himself to the earth and said, "*O Lord,* if I have found favor in your sight, do not pass by your servant. . . . *The Lord said,* "I will surely return to you about this time next year, and Sarah your wife shall have a son." And Sarah was listening at the tent door behind him.

When the Lord appeared to Abraham at the oaks of Mamre, he appeared in the guise of "three men standing in front of him" (Gen. 18.2), yet it is clearly the one Lord who is revealed. In announcing the coming birth of a child to the aged Sarah, they spoke as one. Abraham "saw three and worshipped One," commented Ambrose.
~ Thomas C. Oden. The Living God. San Francisco: HarperSanFrancisco, 1987. p. 191

b. Matt. 3.16-17 - And when *Jesus was baptized*, immediately he went up from the water, and behold, the heavens were opened to him, and *he saw the Spirit of God* descending like a dove and coming to rest on him; and behold, *a voice from heaven said, "This is my beloved Son*, with whom I am well pleased."

3. Threefold Baptismal Formula

Matt. 28.19 - Go therefore and make disciples of all nations, baptizing them *in the name of the Father* and of *the Son* and of *the Holy Spirit*.

4. Threefold Benedictions

a. Num. 6.24-26 - *The Lord* bless you and keep you; *the Lord* make his face to shine upon you and be gracious to you; *the Lord* lift up his countenance upon you and give you peace.

b. 1 Pet. 1.2 - according to the foreknowledge of *God the Father*, in the sanctification of *the Spirit*, for obedience to *Jesus Christ* and for sprinkling with his blood: May grace and peace be multiplied to you.

c. 2 Cor. 13.14 - The grace of the *Lord Jesus Christ* and the love of *God* and the fellowship of the *Holy Spirit* be with you all.

*See Ray Pritchard,
Names of the Holy
Spirit, (Chicago:
Moody Press, 1995),
pp. 36, 59, 158,
173, 196, 207.*

II. The Spirit Who is Lord: The Scriptures Portray the Holy Spirit as Fully God

*We believe in the Holy Spirit, **the Lord** and Life-giver, **who proceeds from the Father and the Son, who along with the Father and Son is worshiped and glorified,** who spoke by the prophets.*

A. The Scriptures directly identify the Holy Spirit as God.

1. Acts 5.3-4

2. Luke 1.35

3. 2 Pet. 1.21

4. 2 Cor. 3.17-18

B. The Spirit possesses divine capacity.

1 Cor. 2.10-11 - these things God has revealed to us through the Spirit. For the Spirit searches everything, even the depths of God. For who knows a person's thoughts except the spirit of that person, which is in him? So also no one comprehends the thoughts of God except the Spirit of God.

C. The Spirit possess divine attributes.

God the Father, God the Son, and God the Holy Spirit are spoken of as distinct persons in the Scriptures and yet each is spoken of as possessing the same attributes of God. (The Spirit is what God is and does what God does.)

1. Divine Nature:

To God the Spirit are ascribed attributes that belong to God alone: omniscience (Isa. 40.13; 1 Cor. 2.10-12), omnipresence (Ps. 139.7-10), omnipotence (Job 33.4; Ps. 104.30; Rom. 15.18,19), eternality (Heb. 9.14).

~ Thomas C. Oden. **Life in the Spirit: Systematic Theology, Vol. 3.**

2. Divine Works:

    a. Reveals God's truth (1 Cor. 2.10; Acts 28.25)

    b. Bestows Spiritual giftings (1 Cor. 12)

    c. Sanctifies from sin (2 Thess. 2.13; 1 Pet. 1.2)

    d. Gives life to the dead (Rom. 8.11)

    e. Governs the Church (Acts 13.2; 15.28)

3. Divine Names:

    a. Spirit of God (Gen. 41.38; 2 Cor. 3.3; Eph. 4.30)

    b. Spirit of Jesus Christ (Acts; 16.7; Rom. 8.9)

    c. Spirit of the Lord (Isa. 61.1; Mic. 2.7)

    d. Spirit of Glory (1 Pet. 4.14)

    e. Spirit of Holiness (Rom. 1.4)

    f. Vindicator of Christ (1 Tim. 3.16)

D. The Spirit possesses divine worthiness.

Matt. 12.32 - Anyone who speaks a word against the Son of Man will be forgiven, but anyone who speaks against the Holy Spirit will not be forgiven, either in this age or in the age to come.

E. The Holy Spirit is a person.

1. A personal description

   a. John 16.13-14

   b. The word for spirit in Greek is neuter and Greek speakers refer to a spirit as an "it." But in John 16.13-14, when Jesus speaks about the Holy Spirit, Jesus does not say, "when the Spirit of truth comes, it will guide you into all truth" but rather "He will guide you into all truth."

2. A personal identity: the Spirit functions as "another like Jesus" which would not be possible if he were not a person.

   a. Jesus spoke of the Spirit's coming as "another (*allon*) Paraclete"* (14.16). This implies that Jesus has already been a paraclete with his disciples, and that the Spirit will come to take his place and continue his ministry with the disciples (George Eldon Ladd, *A Theology of the New Testament*, p. 294).

* *Paraclete comes from the Greek word* **paraklētos** *which literally means "called to one's side," It was commonly used as a legal term that meant an advocate, someone who helped argue the case of another in court. More generally, it could mean anyone who pleads another's cause or intercedes for them (as of the Lord Jesus in 1 John 2.1). It is a term that Jesus applies to the Holy Spirit in John 14.16; 14.26; 15.26 & 16.7. It has been variously translated into English as Helper, Comforter, Advocate, Counselor, and Friend.*

b. John 14.16-18 - *And I will ask the Father, and he will give you another Helper, to be with you forever*, [17] *even the Spirit of truth*, whom the world cannot receive, because it neither sees him nor knows him. You know him, for he dwells with you and will be in you. [18] I will not leave you as orphans; *I will come to you* (cf. John 16.7).

c. In John 16.7-15, Jesus promises that when the Holy Spirit comes he will do in the disciple's lives everything that he himself had done when he was with them personally.

3. The Spirit performs works which require personality.

   a. The Spirit performs the work of counselor/advocate which implies a personal and relational work, i.e. the work of comforting, encouraging, and assisting (see John 16).

   b. The Spirit teaches.

      (1) Luke 12.12

      (2) John 14.26

      (3) John 16.8

      (4) 1 Cor. 2.10

   c. The Spirit wills, directs, and guides.

      (1) 1 Cor. 12.11

      (2) Acts 8.29

      (3) Acts 13.2

      (4) Acts 16.7

      (5) Rom. 8.14

d. The Spirit testifies.

(1) John 15.26

(2) 1 John 5.6.

e. The Spirit intercedes for Christians in prayer, Rom 8.26 (cf. Jude 1.20).

4. The Spirit in Scripture is responded to as a person.

a. He can be grieved and insulted.

(1) Isa. 63.10

(2) Eph. 4.30

(3) Heb. 10.29

b. He can be lied to, Acts 5.3.

5. The Spirit's personality is distinguishable from his power.

a. Acts 10.38 - . . . how God anointed Jesus of Nazareth with the Holy Spirit and with power. He went about doing good and healing all who were oppressed by the devil, for God was with him.

b. 1 Cor. 2.4 - . . . and my speech and my message were not in plausible words of wisdom, but in demonstration of the Spirit and of power.

There are also passages in which the Holy Spirit is distinguished from his own power. Luke 1.35; 4.14; Acts 10.38; Rom. 15.13; 1 Cor. 2.4. Such passages would become tautological, meaningless, and even absurd, if they were interpreted on the principle that the Holy Spirit is merely a power. This can be shown by substituting for the name "Holy Spirit" such a word as "power" or "influence."
~ L. Berkhof. *Systematic Theology.* Grand Rapids, MI: Eerdmans, 1941. p. 96.

III. The Spirit Who Proceeds from the Father and the Son

A. The *Filioque*

There is one small phrase in the Nicene Creed that was not in the original text agreed on by the Church council in 381. That small phrase called the *filioque* [fee-lee-OH-kway], which is Latin for "and the Son," has been a source of great argument in the Church. The Eastern part of the Church which eventually became the Eastern Orthodox Church still uses this original form of the Creed. The Western part of the Church, which eventually became the Roman Catholic Church was fighting heresies which continued to deny that Jesus was truly God. In order to uphold Trinitarian teaching, the phrase "and the Son" was added to make it clear that the Father, the Son, and the Holy Spirit are always interconnected in their actions and essence.

1. The Eastern Church objected saying that only God the Father can be the source of all things. (Although all three persons of the Trinity are co-eternal and co-equal, it is still true that the son is begotten by the Father and not the Father by the Son.) Therefore Scripture says: John 15.26 "But when the Helper comes, whom I will send to you from the Father, the Spirit of truth, who proceeds from the Father, he will bear witness about me.

2. The Western Catholic Church and (eventually the Protestant churches that broke away from them) made the following counter-arguments to Eastern Orthodox churches.

    a. The Holy Spirit is not only called the "Spirit of God" but also the "Spirit of Jesus."

        (1) John 14.16-18

        (2) John 16.13-14

        (3) Gal. 4.6

(4) Phil. 1.19

(5) Rom. 8.9

b. The Holy Spirit is not of the Father only, or the Spirit of the Son only, but he is the Spirit of the Father and the Son. For it is written, "If anyone loves the world, the Spirit of the Father is not in him (1 John 2.15)"; and again it is written: "If anyone, however does not have the Spirit of Christ, he is none of his (Rom. 8.9)." When the Father and the Son are named in this way, the Holy Spirit is understood, of whom the Son himself says in the Gospel, that the Holy Spirit "proceeds from the Father (John 15.26)," and that "He shall receive of mine and shall announce it to you" (John 16.14) (St. Damascus I, 382 A.D.).

c. The Spirit's mission and work proceed from the Father and the Son together. He is a Gift that is given to us jointly by the Father and the Son.

(1) Jesus baptizes believers with the Holy Spirit, Luke 3.16.

(2) Jesus pours out the Holy Spirit promised by the Father, Acts 2.33.

(3) Jesus invites those who are thirsty for the Spirit to come to him and drink, John 7.37-39.

(4) Jesus "breathed out" the Holy Spirit on his disciples, John 20.21-22.

d. Each person in the Trinity must be distinguished theologically. (The Father is not the Son is not the Spirit.)

(1) The Father is of none, neither made, nor created, nor begotten.

(2) The Son is of the Father alone, neither made nor created, but begotten.

(3) The Spirit is of the Father and of the Son, neither made, nor created, nor begotten, but proceeding (part of *The Creed of Athanasius*).

B. The "Bond of Love"

1. St. Augustine, in reflecting on this distinguishing between the members of the Trinity theologically came up with an important description of the Holy Spirit. He called him the "bond of love" between the Father and the Son.

2. The Spirit is closely identified in Scripture with the love of God.

    a. God's love has been poured into our hearts through the Holy Spirit, Rom. 5.5.

    b. God is love, 1 John 4.8.

    c. God is spirit, John 4.24.

    d. If we love one another, God abides in us and his love is perfected in us . . . because he has given us of his Spirit, 1 John 4.12-13.

3. The Spirit of God is the Love which proceeds between the Father and the Son. This "Gift of Love" or "Bond of Love" is a conscious part of the Divine Being.

4. Augustine, therefore, describes the Trinitarian relationship:

   a. "One who loves him who is from himself" (In other words, the Father is the one who loves the Son he begat.) (See Luke 20.13; John 5.20; Col. 1.13; Eph. 1.6; 2 Pet. 1.17.)

   b. "One who loves him from whom he is" (In other words, the Son is the one who loves the Father who begat him.) (See John 5.19; John14.31; John 17.1.)

   c. "And love itself" (In other words, the Holy Spirit is the eternal bond of love between the Father to the Son.) (See Mark 1.10-11; Mark 9.7; John 3.34-35; Gal. 4.6.)

5. The unique role of the Holy Spirit in the Trinity is to be the bond of loving fellowship between the Father and Son.

   a. John 16.13-15

   b. 2 Cor. 13.14

   c. Eph. 4.3

In a mysterious manner Spirit may be said to unite the Father and the Son in love and to proceed as the love between them. . . .Love unites persons who cherish one another, and in God's case love reaches fullness in the third Person, who is loved by Father and Son. . . .The third Person, having no special name like "Father" or "Son" is content with God's generic name of "spirit." It is enough to be known as "bond of love." . . .He delights in the loving relationships of the divine dance and exults in the self-emptying love that binds Father and Son. He delights to introduce creatures to union with God, the dance of the Trinity and the sabbath play of new creation.

~ Clark Pinnock. **Flame of Love**. pp. 38-39.

IV. Who Together with the Father and the Son is Worshiped and Glorified

A. The Logic of the Trinity: The consistent conclusion of all the above arguments is that the Spirit deserves to be reverenced as God.

   1. The Scriptures portray an unbroken unity and equality between the Father, the Son, and the Holy Spirit. Therefore, what is due one member of the Trinity is due to all the others.

   2. Isa. 6.1-3 (cf. Rev. 4.8)

   3. "[In Isaiah 6] The Seraphim utter praise, the whole company of the blessed utter praise, inasmuch as they call God holy, the Son holy, the Spirit holy" (Ambrose, *Of the Holy Spirit*, Bk. III, NPNF, v. 10, p. 151).

B. The Spirit is worshiped in the Church with Trinitarian creeds, prayers, hymns, and benedictions.

The Apostles' letters to the churches (like the Gospels themselves) portrayed God as Father, Son, and Holy Spirit, and established a firm foundation for speaking about God in Trinitarian terms (e.g. 2 Cor. 13.13; Eph. 2.18; 1 Pet. 1.2; Jude 20-21). The early Church borrowed and reflected this language as it prayed and worshiped.

1. The reciting of the Nicene and/or Apostles' Creeds during services.

2. Prayers with endings such as "this we pray through Jesus Christ our Lord, who lives and reigns with You and the Holy Spirit, one God, now and forever Amen."

3. Trinitarian songs/hymns (e.g. *Doxology, Holy, Holy, Holy, Come Thou Almighty King, The Gloria Patri*)

4. Threefold benedictions such as "The blessing of God Almighty, the Father, the Son, and the Holy Spirit, be among you now, and remain with you always. Amen" or "The grace of the Lord Jesus Christ and the love of God and the fellowship of the Holy Spirit be with you all" (2 Cor. 13.14).

Conclusion

The Holy Spirit is the third Person of the one Trinitarian God. He is a distinguishable person in the Godhead who thinks, acts, and loves as fully as the Father and the Son and who fully shares their Divine Nature. The Church has sometimes disagreed about how to define the exact nature of the relationships between the members of the Trinity (e.g. the *filioque*) but all agree on the full deity, personhood, and equality of each member. For both Catholics and Protestants, St. Augustine's description of the Holy Spirit as the "bond of love" between the Father and the Son has proved to be a useful and enduring analogy. In keeping with the witness of Scripture, the Church has always worshiped God as Trinity giving glory to the Father and the to Son and to the Holy Spirit equally and indivisibly.

Segue 1

Student Questions and Response

Please take as much time as you have available to answer these and other questions that the video brought out. We have been working with very difficult ideas about the nature of God and the relationship between the Father, Son, and Spirit. As challenging as these ideas are, they are important because our understanding of God will affect every part of our faith and life. The following questions are meant to help us review and help us understand more fully what we have learned. Be clear and concise in your answers, and where possible, support with Scripture!

1. Why is an understanding of the Trinity foundational to a correct understanding of the Holy Spirit?

2. What evidence do we have that the Spirit is fully God?

3. What evidence do we have that the Spirit is a Divine Person?

4. Why do Protestants and Catholics believe that the Spirit "proceeds from the Father and the Son"?

5. What are the ways in which the Father, Son, and Spirit can be distinguished from each other? (How are they different?)

6. On what biblical basis does the Nicene Creed assert that the Spirit should be "worshiped and glorified"?

The Person of the Holy Spirit

Segment 2: The Life-Giver

Rev. Terry G. Cornett

Summary of Segment 2

This is the second segment of lesson one of this module, entitled, *The Person of the Holy Spirit*. In this segment we will look carefully at a central theme that unites the many activities of the Holy Spirit in the world. We will see that the Spirit gives life to the world through his work in creation and providence. We will examine some of the most common symbols, names, and titles used to describe the Holy Spirit in the Scriptures and explore how each of these contributes to our understanding of the Spirit as Life-giver. Finally, we will conclude with a discussion of how the life-giving ministry of the Spirit brings hope for the future.

Our objective for this segment, *The Life-Giver,* is to enable you to:

- Understand why the theological study of the Holy Spirit is called *Pneumatology.*

- Summarize the Old Testament view of the Spirit of God.

- Use the Scriptures to describe the life-giving role of the Spirit in creating and sustaining the world.

- Identify the major symbols associated with the Holy Spirit in the Scriptures and show how they contribute to our understanding of him as the Life-giver.

- Explain how the names and titles of the Holy Spirit in the Scriptures contribute to our understanding of him as the Life-giver.

- Explain why the ministry of the Spirit is a source of hope.

1

I. The Life-Giver

Video Segment 2
Outline

*We believe in the Holy Spirit, the Lord and **Life-giver**, who proceeds from the Father and the Son, who along with the Father and Son is worshiped and glorified, who spoke by the prophets.*

II. The Powerful Breath of God

A. The study of the doctrine of the Holy Spirit is known as pneumatology.

1. *Pneuma* is the Greek word for "wind or breath or spirit."

2. The Hebrew word *ruach* (which is used in the Old Testament Scriptures) carries the same basic meaning of "wind or breath or spirit."

B. The best description of the Holy Spirit as portrayed in the Old Testament Scriptures would probably be "the powerful breath of God."

1. In the Hebrew Scriptures, God's breath is a powerful force which both destroys (Exod. 15.10; Isa. 11.4) and creates (Ps. 33.6).

. . . .

*The Hebrew word for 'spirit' is **ruach**. The root **r-w-ch**, from which the noun is derived, means primarily "to breathe out through the nose with violence." . . . The word **ruach** stands for hard, strong, violent breathing, as against **neshamah**, which means ordinary, quiet breathing. . . . The word **ruach** is frequently used of the wind; some eighty-seven times in all. Of these thirty-seven speak of the wind as the agent of Jehovah, mostly destructive, and always strong and violent. . . . The **ruach-adonai** [Spirit of the Lord] is the manifestation in human experience of the life-giving, energy-creating power of God. . . . . The **ruach-adonai** cannot be hindered (is not 'straitened'), but is like His word, which shall not return unto Him void, but will accomplish that which He pleases.*

~ N. H. Snaith. Chapter VII, "The Spirit of God."
The Distinctive Ideas of the Old Testament. pp. 143-158.

. . . .

2. Old Testament Judaism understood the Holy Spirit to be "the power of God in action." That power might be demonstrated as:

a. Strength in battle (as when the Wind of God parts the Red Sea or when the Judges are empowered in their fight against Israel's enemies)

b. Various kinds of wisdom (as with the craftsmen at the Tabernacle or Joseph or Daniel having special gifts for the administration of Government).

c. Prophetic utterances (such as those given by Jeremiah or Ezekiel).

III. The Power that Gives Life

A. The Spirit is intimately involved in the creation of the world.

Gen. 1.1-2 - In the beginning, God created the heavens and the earth. The earth was without form and void, and darkness was over the face of the deep. And the Spirit of God was hovering over the face of the waters.

1. The Spirit's "hovering"

   a. The Hebrew word translated "hovering" (*rachaph*) suggests careful tending (cf. Deut. 32.11). The Spirit of God tended the new creation preparing it to move from formlessness to order, from darkness to light.

      Gen. 1.2 - "with a *divine wind*"

   b. The Spirit's role in physical creation is similar to the Spirit's role in "new creation" (salvation) (see John 3).

      John 3.8 - The *wind* blows where it wishes, and you hear its sound, but you do not know where it comes from or where it goes. So it is with everyone who·is born of the Spirit.

2. The Spirit is the Breath of God which brings humanity to life.

   a. The first human being, Gen. 2.7

In the OT the spirit (rûah) of Yahweh is God's power in action. . . . A term for both breath blown out and wind blowing . . . rûah has vivid and awesome association when used of God's energy let loose. It is so used in nearly 100 of its nearly 400 OT appearances.
~"Holy Spirit." *New Dictionary of Theology*. Downers Grove, IL/Leicester, England: Inter-Varsity Press, 1988. p. 316.

See Ray Pritchard, Names of the Holy Spirit. *Chicago: Moody Press, 1995. pp. 11, 13, 34.*

b. All human beings, Job 33.4, 6

B. The Spirit is intimately involved with sustaining life in the world.

1. The Doctrine of Providence

a. Definition: Providence comes from the word *provide*. Through his providence God sustains, governs, and protects the life that he gave the earth and guides it toward the end for which it was created.

> *The root meaning of Providence is to foresee, or to provide. The question of providence concerns how God **thinks ahead** to care for all creatures.... God's providing looks ahead for needs as yet unrecognized by creatures. But more than simply foresight, providence has to do with the active, daily caring of God for the world in its hazards.*
>
> ~ Thomas C. Oden. **The Living God**. p. 271.

b. The work of the Holy Spirit in providence: the Life-giver.

(1) The Spirit is at work to create, renew, and provide for all the forms of life that exist within the created order.

(2) OT: Ps. 104.29-30; Isa. 32.14-15

(3) NT: John 6.63; Rom. 8.2, 6, 11

2. The scriptural symbols of the Holy Spirit reveal him as Life-giver.

a. Water - the source of life.

(1) Isa. 44.2-4a

Throughout the universe the immense forces that are at work in suns, stars, and galaxies are energized by the Spirit of God. All energy and power are there by virtue of the divine Spirit.
~ J. Rodman Williams

(2) John 7.37-39

(3) John 4.14

(4) 1 Cor. 6.11 (cf. Titus 3.5)

(5) Rev. 22.17

*See Ray Pritchard,
**Names of the Holy
Spirit**. Chicago:
Moody Press, 1995.
pp. 57, 69, 77,
100, 187.*

b. Oil - the sustaining of life

In biblical times, olive oil was used for both food and medicine as well as for fuel for lamps which lit the house. It was so vital to daily life that it became a symbol for prosperity. One could not think of oil without thinking of healing, security, and abundance. It sustained life.

Oil as an image of the Holy Spirit, took on an even more important symbolic role because of the biblical practice of anointing. Prophets (1 Kings 19.16), priests (Exod. 28.41), and kings (2 Sam. 2.4; 1 Kings 1.34) were anointed with oil to set them apart for ministry. This pouring on of oil was a symbol which showed visibly that the person was having the Holy Spirit poured out on them. The anointing with oil shows that God had chosen and equipped a person to minister life, health, security, and abundance to his people. In the Old Testament Scriptures this special anointing (empowerment) of the Holy Spirit was usually limited to those who served as prophets, priests, or kings. In the New Testament, every believer in Christ, receives an anointing of the Spirit to be a minster of life to others.

(1) 1 Sam. 16.13a (cf. Isa. 61.1).

(2) Luke 4.18

(3) 2 Cor. 1.21-22

(4) 1 John 2.20 & 27 (compare with John 14.26)

Ibid. p. 19.

c. Fire - the protection (purification) of life.

The ancient world did not have microbe killing medicines. The primary agent for cleansing and purification was fire. Garbage was burned to keep it from becoming a breeding ground for disease (Lev. 8.17). When disease had broken out, burning the infected person's clothes was often the only way to stop the disease from spreading (Lev. 13.47-59). Fire also refined metals and made them pure and useful (Mal. 3.2-3).

Throughout the Scriptures God uses the symbol of fire to speak about the purification of his people. The prophet Isaiah, for example, speaks about a day "when the Lord shall have washed away the filth of the daughters of Zion and cleansed the bloodstains of Jerusalem from its midst by a spirit of judgment and by a spirit of burning" (Isa. 4.4).

(1) Matt. 3.11-12

(2) Acts 2.3-4

(3) 1 Thess. 5.19

Ibid. pp. 40, 110.

(4) The Holy Spirit as the fire of God, constantly purifies the Church, protecting it from the infection that sin might bring.

d. The Dove - the symbol of new life

In Genesis chapter 8, when God has destroyed all life on the earth because of sin, only Noah, his kinfolk, and a group of animals remain alive on the ark. As they wait for the waters to subside, they send out a dove to see if it can find dry land. Initially, just like the Holy Spirit at creation, the dove "hovers over the waters" but cannot find a resting place and returns to the ark. It is sent out a second time and returns with an olive leaf indicating that the water level is lowering. The third time it is sent out it does not return and Noah knows that dry land has appeared and it is safe to come out of the Ark and start life on the earth again. In the Noah story, the dove becomes the symbol of new creation and new hope for the earth.

(1) When God sends Jesus to the earth he also enters the waters, not of the flood, but of the Jordan River in baptism, Luke 3.22.

(2) This incident is so important that it is recorded in all four of the Gospel accounts. The appearance of the Holy Spirit as a dove reminds the Jewish audience who sees Jesus baptized that, like Noah, this man is beloved of God and the means of new hope and new creation.

Ibid. p. 79.

3. The scriptural names and titles of the Holy Spirit reveal him as Life-giver.

   a. He is called the Spirit of Truth (John 14.16-17; 15.26; 16.13). He is the one who teaches us the words of life.

   b. His is called the Spirit of Holiness (Rom. 1.4). He is the one who enables us to overcome sin and death.

   c. He is called the Spirit of Grace (Heb. 10.29). He is the one who freely brings new life to those who could not obtain it through their own efforts.

   d. He is called "the Spirit of Life" (Rom. 8.2). He has the ministry of bringing life and is the source of resurrection.

   Ibid. pp. 105, 123, 127, 131, 191.

C. "Where there is Life there is hope": the results of the Spirit's life-giving ministry

Rom. 15.13 - May the God of hope fill you with all joy and peace in believing, *so that by the power of the Holy Spirit you may abound in hope.*

1. The Spirit's ministry of hope flows from his critical role in the life-giving renewal of all things.

   a. Ezek. 36.6-37.28

   b. Matt. 19.28 (cf. Titus 3.5)

2. The Spirit as the in-breaking presence of the "Age to Come"

   a. The firstfruits of a renewed creation, Rom. 8.23-24

   b. The guarantee of resurrection and eternal life, 2 Cor. 5.1-5

   c. The downpayment on the rule of Christ in the Age to Come, Eph. 1.13-14, 19-21.

Conclusion

[The] Spirit is at work in history, first bringing humankind into existence and then moving it toward the goal of union [with God]. Spirit is the power released to bring the divine plans to completion. He is Spirit of creation and new creation, concerned with creating community and bringing about the kingdom. Spirit is the power by which this present age will be transformed into the kingdom and which ever works to bring about ultimate fulfillment . . . The scope is breathtaking. God's breath is on the whole creation–we live and move and have our being in an ocean of love.

~ Clark Pinnock. **Flame of Love**. p. 61.

Segue 2

Student Questions and Response

The following questions were designed to help you review the material in the second video segment. They focus on the Spirit's identity as one who gives life. Be clear and concise in your answers, and where possible, support with Scripture!

1. How are the Old and New Testament ideas about the Spirit of God alike? How are they different?
2. What is the Spirit's role in creation? What does this suggest about his role in the salvation of believers (new creation)?
3. What is providence? What part does the Spirit play in God's care of the world?
4. What are the key symbols of the Holy Spirit in Scripture? How do these contribute to our understanding of the Spirit as the one who gives life?
5. What are biblical titles of the Holy Spirit that emphasize his life-giving ministry?
6. How does the ministry of the Spirit bring hope to all believers?

1

CONNECTION

Summary of Key Concepts

This lesson focuses upon the person of the Holy Spirit. In it we discussed the following ideas:

- The Holy Spirit is the Third person of the one Trinitarian God.
- Like the Father and the Son, the Holy Spirit is a Divine person who relates to God's people in personal ways (speaking, acting, guiding, teaching, etc.).
- In the same way that Jesus came alongside his disciples during his earthly ministry, the Holy Spirit now comes alongside all Christians, teaching, guiding, and protecting them on Jesus' behalf.
- The Spirit proceeds from the Father and the Son. He is the full expression of their love and the one who is sent into the world as a gift of love.
- Jesus commands his followers to baptize God's people in the Name of the Father, the Son, and the Holy Spirit. The Apostles address and bless God's people in the Name of the Father, the Son, and the Holy Spirit. The heavenly creatures in God's throne room worship him in Triune address,

crying "Holy, Holy, "Holy" (Isa. 6.3; Rev. 4.8). The Church follows in their footsteps, worshiping and glorifying God as Father, Son, and Holy Spirit.

↤ The doctrine of the Holy Spirit in theology is known as pneumatology which comes from the Greek word *pneuma* which means spirit, breath, or wind.

↤ God the Holy Spirit is portrayed in Scripture as the Life-giver who is both the Creator and Sustainer of all life.

↤ The images and symbols used for the Holy Spirit in the Bible reinforce the idea that the Holy Spirit both gives and sustains all life.

↤ The scriptural titles of the Holy Spirit demonstrate the scope of his life-giving ministry and even directly name him as "the Spirit of Life."

↤ The life-giving mission of the Holy Spirit means that he is the source of hope for individuals, for the Church, and for the world.

Student Application and Implications

Now is the time for you to discuss with your fellow students your questions about the material we have covered in this lesson "The Person of the Holy Spirit." Even the most abstract theology is not intended to be an "academic exercise." Theological truth is meant to affect our lives. The most important part of asking and answering questions about the Holy Spirit, is discovering how God wants to change us through what we have learned. What particular questions do you have in light of the material you have just studied? Maybe some of the questions below might help you form your own, more specific and critical questions.

* One of the most consistent shared characteristics of "cults" is that they teach the wrong thing about who God is. (If someone misrepresents God true nature as revealed in Scripture, they cannot help but misrepresent God's work in the world.) What kind of errors might result from thinking wrongly about the person of the Holy Spirit?

* What are the implications of the fact that the Spirit is sent as the *paraclete*; the one called alongside us be the living presence of Jesus in our midst?

* How does the description of the Holy Spirit as the "bond of love" between the Father and the Son affect our understanding of the Spirit's role in our own lives and church communities?

1

* What are some of the practical ways in which our churches can "worship and glorify the Spirit" along with the Father and the Son?

* Is there any significance to the fact that the Hebrew and Greek words for Spirit also mean "breath" or "wind"? What do these closely related concepts tell us about the Spirit's work?

* How has the Holy Spirit operated as the Life-giver in your own experience? What are the implications of his life-giving power for the way we view ministry?

* Which of the scriptural symbols of the Holy Spirit have been particularly important in your own life? How have they helped you understand the Holy Spirit? How have they affected your understanding of Christian leadership?

* As Christians who are indwelt by the Holy Spirit, we often think of the Spirit's work in very personal terms: the Spirit is the one who lives in me and helps me know and obey God. Is it common for you to also think of the Holy Spirit as the one who is caring for the whole creation and who is preparing the world for the coming reign of Christ? (Explain your answer).

CASE STUDIES

◄ **1**

Ready to Give an Answer

You are teaching a bible study at your church on the doctrine of the Holy Spirit and you remind your students that he is rightly called the Lord and Life-giver. Sue, a visitor who has come to the study only a few times, perks right up when she hears your comment. Sue says, "I usually attend the Unity Church down the street and they gave me a book that talks about that very thing." She pulls out the book and flips through it until she finds these quotes, "God is Spirit, or the creative energy which is the cause of all visible things. . . . God is not a being or person having life, intelligence, love, power. . . . God is that invisible, intangible, but very real, something we call life. . . . Each rock, tree, animal, everything visible, is a manifestation of the one Spirit - God - differing only in degree of manifestation; and each of the numberless modes of manifestation, or individualities, however insignificant, contains the whole" (*Lessons In Truth*, H. Emilie Cady, published by The Unity School of Christianity, pp. 18, 19-20). You realize immediately that she has been studying with a group that does not have a correct doctrine of God or the

Trinity. What will you say to her, and to the Bible study group, as you respond to the quote she read?

Searching for Clarity

2 Carlos is a new believer in Christ who is trying to understand what the Bible teaches about the Holy Spirit. He says, "It is easy for me to understand who Jesus is. I can read the stories about him in Scripture and know exactly what he said and did. When I put my trust in Christ for salvation, I felt just like Peter did when he told the Lord that he couldn't go anywhere else because Jesus had 'the words of eternal life.' But the Holy Spirit seems very mysterious. I can't seem to imagine what he is like and I am not sure how I am supposed to have a relationship with him. Can you help me figure it out?" How can you use Carlos' current understanding of Jesus to help him understand the Holy Spirit?

Leading Trinitarian Worship

3 Many Christian churches follow the Church calendar, setting aside special days and seasons to emphasize important events in the Gospels and the Book of Acts. Suppose your church was celebrating Pentecost Sunday* for the very first time. In your tradition, are there songs, benedictions, actions, decorations, colors, symbols, readings, spiritual giftings, or other forms of worship that particularly focus on the person and work of the Holy Spirit? If you were put in charge of that Pentecost Sunday worship service, what things could you plan that would help your congregation joyfully worship and glorify God the Holy Spirit?

Pentecost Sunday is the 7th Sunday after Easter, and is traditionally a service which remembers and celebrates the coming of the Holy Spirit in fulfillment of the prophecy of Joel (Joel 2.28-32) and the promise of Jesus (John 14.16-17; 16.7; Acts 1.8).

Restatement of the Lesson's Thesis

The Holy Spirit is the Lord; the third person of the one Trinitarian God. He is a distinguishable person in the Godhead who thinks, acts, and loves as fully as the Father and the Son and who fully shares their Divine Nature. As Lord, he is given worship and glory along with the Father and the Son. The Holy Spirit is the Life-giver: the Creator and Sustainer of all life. He is given symbols and titles in

Scripture which help us more fully understand his life-giving work. He is also the one who gives new life (regenerates); first through the new birth by which people are made new creations in Christ; and one day still future when he gives birth to a new heavens and a new earth, the home of righteousness.

If you are interested in pursuing some of the ideas of *The Person of the Holy Spirit*, you might want to give these books a try:

Bickersteth, Edward Henry. *The Trinity*. Grand Rapids, MI: Kregel Publications, 1977.

Saint Basil. *On the Holy Spirit*. Crestwood, NY: St. Vladimir's Seminary Press, 1980. Also available as an on-line text at the following web sites:

- www.newadvent.org/fathers/3201000.html

- www.monachos.net/patristics/basil/on_holy_spirit_a.shtml

Resources and Bibliographies

Now is the time to try to nail down this high theology by applying it in actual ministry. What truth from the lesson did God quicken to your own heart? What particular situation comes to mind when you think about training people to understand the doctrine of the Holy Spirit? What part of this lesson will you think and pray about through the upcoming week. Reflecting on the person of the Holy Spirit has been challenging and difficult work in the history of the Church. You are called to enter into this long stream of theological reflection and see the practical implications for those that you lead and teach. Fortunately, you can ask the Holy Spirit himself to come and help you understand these deep truths and give you direct guidance as to how they need to affect your life and ministry. Do not neglect to ask the Spirit to illuminate the Scriptures we have studied. He will make clear their meaning and usefulness. The prayer that is located in the next section is a good way to get started on this.

Ministry Connections

Holy Spirit of God, "open my eyes to see wonderful things in your word." My understanding is limited, Your understanding is infinite. I "see through a glass darkly," You search the thoughts of the one "who dwells in unapproachable light." Teach me the meaning of the Scriptures you inspired. Illumine my mind to know the truth and to see what you want me to do because of it. Empower me to fulfill my

Counseling and Prayer

ministry calling. Give me the wisdom to lead others to a true knowledge of You. All this I pray through Jesus Christ, who lives and reigns with You and the Father Almighty, one God, forever blessed. Amen.

Scripture Memory

Romans 8.15-17

Reading Assignment

To prepare for class, please visit *www.tumi.org/books* to find next week's reading assignment, or ask your mentor.

Other Assignments

You will be quizzed on the content (the video content) of this lesson next week. Make sure that you spend time covering your notes, especially focusing on the main ideas of the lesson. Read the assigned reading, and summarize each reading with no more than a paragraph or two for each. In this summary please give your best understanding of what you think was the main point in each of the readings. Do not be overly concerned about giving detail; simply write out what you consider to be the main point discussed in that section of the book. Please bring these summaries to class next week. (Please see the *Reading Completion Sheet* at the end of this lesson.)

Looking Forward to the Next Lesson

In our next lesson we will focus on the prophetic work of the Holy Spirit. We will talk about the prophetic Word as the basis for knowing God and examine the role of the Spirit in inspiring and illuminating the Scriptures. We will emphasize that the Spirit is not only prophetic in his revelation of God's Word but is equally the one who applies the prophetic Word to the human heart. We will look at the ministry of the Holy Spirit in regard to convicting people of sin and bringing them to repentance. In all of this we will affirm our complete dependence on the Spirit for any saving knowledge of God and any empowerment for obedience to his Word.

Name _____

Date _____

For each assigned reading, write a brief summary (one or two paragraphs) of the author's main point. (For additional readings, use the back of this sheet.)

Reading 1

Title and Author: _____ Pages _____

Reading 2

Title and Author: _____ Pages _____

The Prophetic Work of the Holy Spirit

Lesson Objectives

Welcome in the strong name of Jesus Christ! After your reading, study, discussion, and application of the materials in this lesson, you will be able to:

- Describe the biblical concept of prophecy.

- Understand that all Scripture is a "prophetic" word from the Spirit of God.

- See that all prophecy involves "forthtelling" a message from God, while some prophecy also involves "foretelling" a future event in God's plan.

- Demonstrate from Scripture that prophecy is a ministry given to women as well as men.

- Prove from Scripture that prophecy comes through the ministry of the Holy Spirit.

- Verify the biblical claim that the Holy Spirit is the author of the Scriptures.

- Define the doctrines of *inspiration* and *illumination* and explain the relationship between them.

- Recognize that human beings are deceived about their sinful condition (its seriousness and consequences) and unwilling and unable to truly seek God and his righteousness.

- Explain the meaning of conviction and describe the Spirit's role in bringing people to a knowledge of their sinful condition.

- Define the key Hebrew and Greek words for repentance.

- Describe the kinds of change that accompany true biblical repentance.

- Demonstrate from the Scriptures that repentance is produced by the work of the Holy Spirit.

Attending to the Prophetic Word

Read 2 Peter 1.16-21. The Apostle Peter was firmly convinced that what he had seen and heard on the Mount of Transfiguration was the sure fulfillment of the prophetic testimony about Christ found in the Old Testament Scriptures. For Peter, the words of the Hebrew Scriptures are words that come directly from the Spirit of God himself. He says that the prophets who wrote the Scriptures were "carried along by the Holy Spirit." (The word translated "carried along" is the same Greek word use in Acts 27.17 to describe a ship that is being driven forward by the wind in its sails). In Peter's understanding, the Holy Spirit carried the prophets along as surely as wind carries a ship. The ancient Christian theologian, Athenagoras, captured the same idea when he wrote that ". . . [Prophets] spoke the things with which they were inspired. The Spirit operated through them just as a flute player breathes into a flute."

As those who have placed our faith in Christ, we firmly believe that the Holy Spirit did, indeed, speak through the prophets. We believe that in the Scriptures we have found a form of truth that did not have its origins in human ideas but instead came from the mind of God himself. The prophetic word is, as Peter says, "a lamp shining in a dark place" and we are to give our full attention to it. We truly believe that every part of the study of theology that we are engaged in should be nothing more than an attempt to give our full attention to the Word of God that has been breathed out by his Spirit. As we come to our lesson, let's begin by asking God the Holy Spirit to illuminate our minds so that we not only hear, but that we may also fully understand the truths of God's prophetic word. We pray along with the Psalmist, "Open my eyes, that I may behold wondrous things out of your law" (Ps. 119.18).

After reciting and/or singing the Nicene Creed (located in the Appendix), pray the following prayer:

> *Almighty God, to you all hearts are open, all desires known, and from you no secrets are hid: Cleanse the thoughts of our hearts by the inspiration of your Holy Spirit, that we may perfectly love you, and worthily magnify your holy Name; through Christ our Lord. Amen.*

~ **The Book of Common Prayer**.
New York, NY: The Church Hymnal Corporation, 1979. p. 355.

Quiz

Put away your notes, gather up your thoughts and reflections, and take the quiz for Lesson 1, *The Person of the Holy Spirit.*

Scripture Memorization Review

Review with a partner, write out and/or recite the text for last class session's assigned memory verse: Romans 8.5-17.

Assignments Due

Turn in your summary of the reading assignment for last week, that is, your brief response and explanation of the main points that the authors were seeking to make in the assigned reading (Reading Completion Sheet).

Making God Known

How do we know things? How do we know with certainty that a chair is red, or that there is such a thing as red, or even such a thing as color? In the modern age, not even looking at something with our own eyes is completely reliable because technology is affecting our ability to know what is real and what is not. Films and photographs can be altered so seamlessly that even so-called "experts" are not always sure that it has happened. The old saying, "seeing is believing" is rapidly becoming untrue.

Epistemology is the academic discipline that tries to define what knowledge is and how we can obtain it and evaluate it. There are many ways to know things. For example:

- Observation and testing - This is the way that scientists know things.

- Reason, logic, and deduction - This is the way philosophers know things.

- Experiences, senses, hunches, insight, and imagination - This is the way artists know things.

Each of these ways of knowing has certain strengths and weaknesses but all of these have some severe limitations when it comes to knowing God. (What are some of those limits? Can we know God through science, philosophy, or art? Why or why not?)

Karl Barth says: "The attempt is made [by the Church] to speak of God with the intention that others shall hear of Him. This attempt and intention are as such impossible. God does not belong to the world. Therefore, he does not belong to the series of objects for which we have categories and words. . ." (*Church Dogmatics, Vol. I.2, The Doctrine of the Word of God*).

What does 1 Corinthians 2.13 have to say about this problem? What is the role of the Holy Spirit in knowing God. Can we know God apart from the special revealing work of the Holy Spirit? Why or Why not?

Amazing Grace, How Sweet the Sound, that Saved a Wretch Like Me

In the second part of this lesson, we will be discussing the role of the Holy Spirit in convicting people of their sinfulness and drawing them to faith and repentance. How did this happen in your own life? What persuaded you that you were truly guilty before God? How did the Holy Spirit convince you to acknowledge your sin and what happened following that time of confession?

The Spirit of Prophecy

Christians of all denominations acknowledge that the Spirit's most important prophetic work is the inspiration of the Scriptures. The Scriptures are the source and measuring rod of all authoritative knowledge about God and his will. When Christians speak about the Spirit's prophetic work today, however, different Christian traditions differ in their emphasis. Some equate prophetic ministry with preaching (the Spirit's gift to illuminate the prophetic text) while others see a continuing role for prophetic words which guide and direct the Church (within the bounds of Scripture). Which of these two approaches more closely describes your own church's experience?

The Prophetic Work of the Holy Spirit

Segment 1: The Spirit Who Spoke by the Prophets

Rev. Terry G. Cornett

Summary of Segment 1

We can know the Living God only because he chooses to reveal himself to us. It is the Spirit of God who puts the knowledge of God into human words and makes them known to the prophets. The Spirit of God both gives us the Scriptures and enables us to understand and believe the truths they teach. Apart from the Spirit's work, no person would either want to seek God or be able to discover what he is like.

Our objective for this segment, *The Spirit Who Spoke by the Prophets*, is to enable you to:

- Describe the biblical concept of prophecy.

- Understand that all Scripture is a "prophetic" word from the Spirit of God.

- See that all prophecy involves "forthtelling" a message from God, while some prophecy also involves "foretelling" a future event in God's plan.

- Demonstrate from Scripture that prophecy is a ministry given to women as well as men.

- Prove from Scripture that prophecy comes through the ministry of the Holy Spirit.

- Verify the biblical claim that the Holy Spirit is the author of the Scriptures.

- Define the doctrines of inspiration and illumination and explain the relationship between them.

In this first segment we will explore the biblical doctrine of prophetic inspiration. The Nicene Creed reminds us that this doctrine relates directly to the ministry of the Holy Spirit when it says that the Spirit is the one "who spoke by the prophets."

I. What Is Prophecy?

A. Definition: prophecy is a way of knowing truth that comes by direct revelation from God.

1. The Greek word *prophētēs* (prophet):

a. *Pro* (which means "before" or "for")

b. *Phēmi* (which means "to speak")

c. The prophet is one who speaks for someone or speaks before someone (that is, someone who proclaims a message). Therefore, the traditional definition of a biblical prophet is "one who speaks for God to the people."

2. Prophecy is a message that comes directly from God.

a. Jer. 1.9

b. W. E. Vine says that a prophet is: "One who speaks forth openly. . . a proclaimer of the divine message. . . . one upon whom the Spirit of God rested . . . one, to whom and through whom, God speaks" (*Vines Complete Expository Dictionary of Old and New Testament Words*, p. 493).

3. All Scripture is prophetic, that is, a revelation of truth directly from God through inspired writers.

There are three Hebrew words used of the prophet: nābî, rō'eh and hōzeh. The first of these is always translated 'prophet'; the second, which is, in form, an active participle of the verb "to see" is translated "seer"; the third, also an active principle of another verb 'to see', is unfortunately without distinctive English equivalent and is translated either 'prophet' (e.g. Isa. 30.10) or 'seer' (e.g. 1 Chron. 29.29).
~ "Prophecy." New Bible Dictionary, 2nd ed. p. 976.

B. Dealing with misconceptions about prophecy

1. Misconception #1: All prophecy predicts the future.

    a. *Some* prophecy predicts the future. For example:

        (1) Warnings of God's coming judgment on sin

        (2) Unfolding revelation about God's plans, especially his plan to send the Messiah (e.g. Isa. 11.1; Mic. 5.2)

    b. Predictive prophecies are very significant but nonetheless they make up a relatively small amount of the total prophetic word we call the Scriptures.

    c. Gordon Fee and Douglas Stuart say *"Less than 2 percent of Old Testament prophecy is Messianic. Less than 5 percent describes the New Covenant. Less than 1 percent describes events yet to come."*

    d. Most prophecy is a revelation about God's person, about his character, about his relationship to his chosen people, and about his purposes for all humanity rather than a prediction of future events. To use a classic theological distinction, *all* prophecy is forthtelling, while some prophecy is also foretelling.

2. Misconception #2: Prophecy is only found in one part of Scripture.

    a. The Hebrew Scriptures were arranged in three divisions - the Law, the Prophets, and the Writings.

2

b. The writings characterized as "The Prophets" are largely made up of oracles given by recognized prophets. These prophecies particularly focus on calling disobedient Israel back to pure devotion to Yahweh.

c. The author of the Law is Israel's greatest prophet.

  (1) Moses wrote the books of the Law (Torah), not the prophetic books.

  (2) Moses is the key prophet of the Old Testament. He stands as the fundamental measuring rod of all prophetic ministry that followed him and is himself a pattern for the prophetic ministry of the Messiah.

  (3) Deut. 34.10

  (4) Deut. 18.15 (cf. Acts 3.22; 7.37).

d. Anyone who writes under divine inspiration from the Spirit of God is writing prophetically even though what he or she is writing may not be placed in the section of Scripture known as "prophetic books." Again, in the broadest sense, all Scripture is prophecy, not just certain sections within it, because all of it is truth that comes by direct revelation from God.

3. Misconception #3: All prophets are men.

a. The Scriptures record numerous women prophets.

  (1) Miriam, the sister of Moses, Exod. 15.20

  (2) Deborah, Judges 4.4

  (3) Huldah, 2 Chron. 34.22

  (4) Anna, Luke 2.36

The broad usage of the term [prophet] explains why the patriarch Abram (Gen. 20.7), the priest Aaron (Exod. 7.1), and the singer Jeduthun (1 Chron. 25.3) were all called prophets even though the Scriptures contain no record of their call to prophetic office.
~ International Standard Bible Encyclopedia,
Vol. 3. p. 986.

We also find examples of women among the false prophets of Israel (Neh. 6.14; Ezek. 13.17). Gender is neither a hindrance to godly prophetic ministry nor a guarantee of it!

(5) The four daughters of Philip the Evangelist, Acts 21.9

b. The Scriptures themselves identify the outpouring of the Holy Spirit with prophetic ministry that is freely available to both men and women.

(1) Joel's prediction (Joel 2.28-29)

(2) The Pentecost fulfillment

c. Acts 2.17-18 - And in the last days it shall be, God declares, that I will pour out my Spirit on all flesh, and your sons and your daughters shall prophesy, and your young men shall see visions, and your old men shall dream dreams; [18] even on my male servants and female servants in those days I will pour out my Spirit, and they shall prophesy.

II. The Holy Spirit is the Source of Prophetic Speech.

A. Prophecy is closely linked to the Spirit of God coming upon a person.

1. Old Testament

a. The seventy Elders of Israel, Num. 11.25

b. The Prophet Ezekiel, Ezek. 11.5

c. The Prophet Micah, Micah 3.8

d. The long line of prophets that God sent to his people, Zech. 7.12

     e. Saul's messengers and Saul himself, 1 Sam. 19.20, 23-24

     f. A future generation of God's people, Joel 2.28-29

2. New Testament

     a. According to Paul, the Holy Spirit spoke through Isaiah, Acts 28.25-26.

     b. Those in the Upper Room at Pentecost, Acts 2.16-18

     c. John the Baptist's disciples at Ephesus, Acts 19.6

     d. The example of Jesus, Luke 4.18; John 3.34

B. Prophecy is described as a gift from the Holy Spirit.

. . . .

All may agree that there appears no new revelation to be expected concerning God in Christ. But there appears to be no good reason why the living God, who both speaks and acts (in contrast to dead idols), cannot use the gift of prophecy to give particular local guidance to a church, nation or individual, or to warn or encourage by way of prediction as well as by reminders, in full accord with the written word of Scripture, by which all such utterances must be tested. Certainly the NT does not see it as the job of the prophet to be a doctrinal innovator, but to deliver the word the Spirit gives him in line with the truth once for all delivered to the saints (Jude 3), to challenge and encourage our faith.

~ J. P. Baker. "Prophecy." **New Bible Dictionary**, 2nd ed.
J. D. Douglas and others, eds.
Leicester, England-Downers Grove, IL: InterVarsity Press, 1982. p. 985.

1. 1 Cor. 12.4-11

2. Rom. 12

3. 1 Thess. 5.19-21

C. The Old and New Testament Scriptures are inspired by the Holy Spirit.

   1. The Doctrine of Inspiration.

      a. Definition: By inspiration of Scripture, we mean that supernatural influence of the Holy Spirit upon the Scripture writers which rendered their writings an accurate record of the revelation or which resulted in what they wrote actually being the Word of God (Millard Erickson, *Introducing Christian Doctrine*, p. 61).

      b. The Scriptures themselves testify that they are authored by the Holy Spirit.

        (1) The Spirit spoke by David, 2 Sam. 23.1-2.

        (2) The Old Testament prophets were carried along by the Spirit rather than their own will, 2 Pet. 1.20-21.

        (3) Jesus affirmed that David spoke by the Holy Spirit, Matt. 22.43.

        (4) The early Christian believers affirmed that David spoke by the Holy Spirit, Acts 4.25.

        (5) Paul says that all Scripture is "breathed out" by God, 2 Tim. 3.16.

        (6) The Old Testament Scriptures are quoted as an authentic voice of the Holy Spirit, Heb. 3.7.

2

2. The Doctrine of Illumination

   a. Definition: Illumination is a work of the Holy Spirit which enables the readers of Scripture to grasp its meaning for their own life and times.

   b. The Scriptures testify that God's revelation can only be understood through the illuminating work of the Holy Spirit.

     (1) The Spirit is sent to remind believers of what Jesus taught and to teach them what it means, John 14.26 (cf. Isa. 59.21).

     (2) The Spirit guides believers into truth by helping believers discern what truly comes from God, John 16.13-15 (cf. 1 John 2.26-27).

     (3) The Spirit not only chooses the words of Scriptures but he also interprets them and gives believers the ability to discern their meaning, 1 Cor. 2.9-14 (cf. 2 Cor. 4.3-4).

3. There is an ongoing relationship between inspiration and illumination.

   a. In *inspiration*, the Spirit moves upon a writer to produce a text that truly reveals God's mind, will, and heart.

   b. In *illumination*, the Holy Spirit moves upon a reader (or hearer) of the Scriptures to help that person correctly understand God's mind, will, and heart.

   c. Without this illuminating work of the Holy Spirit, prophecy would fall upon deaf ears.

*Commenting on the Spirit's role in illumination, John Miley says, "Such illumination is a familiar idea of Scripture. As a part of inspiration, the operation may be similar to that of Christ when he opened the minds of his disciples that they might understand the Scriptures (Luke 24.45). They were thus able to understand truths previously revealed. In like manner theirs must be divine illumination. . . of revelation for the proper reception and apprehension of its truths" (**Systematic Theology**, Vol. 2, p. 481).*

d. [The Apostle Paul] prays, "that the God of the Lord Jesus Christ, the Father of Glory, may give you the spirit of wisdom and revelation (Eph. 1.17). . . . David had the law, comprehending in it all the wisdom that could be desired, and yet not contented with this, he prays, "Open mine eyes that I may behold wondrous things out of thy law" (Ps. 119.18). . . because whatever is not illuminated by his Spirit is wholly darkness. . . If we confess that what we ask of God is lacking to us. . . no man can hesitate to acknowledge that he is able to understand the mysteries of God, only in so far as illuminated by his grace (John Calvin, *Institutes*, II.2.21).

Conclusion

» Prophecy is a way of knowing truth that comes by direct revelation from God.

» A prophet is one who speaks for God to the people.

» All prophecy is "forthtelling" a divine message. *Sometimes* this divine message involves a "foretelling" of future events.

» Prophets may be women as well as men.

» All true prophecy is given through the ministry of the Holy Spirit.

» The Holy Spirit inspired the Scriptures. Inspiration is the work of the Holy Spirit that reveals a divine message and causes God's truth to be accurately portrayed in human words.

» Illumination is the work of the Holy Spirit which enables the readers of Scripture to grasp its meaning for their own life and times. God's revelation can only be understood and believed through the illuminating work of the Holy Spirit.

Segue 1

Student Questions and Response

Please take as much time as you have available to answer these and other questions that the video brought out. Jesus said, "It is written, 'Man shall not live by bread alone, but by every word that comes from the mouth of God.'" Matt. 4.4. Those who lead the people of God must be absolutely convinced that the Scriptures are the foundation and the measuring rod for everything we know about God and his will.

Equally, Christian leaders must know how to hear the voice of the Spirit today as he instructs us in the meaning of the Scriptures he inspired and leads us to faithfully obey Christ's teachings. Be clear and concise in your answers to the following questions, and where possible, support with Scripture!

1. What is the broad definition of prophecy? What is a good definition of a prophet?

2. What misconceptions do people frequently have about prophecy? What problems might these misconceptions cause?

3. Prophecy may involve *forthtelling* or *foretelling*. What is the difference between them? How do they relate to each other?

4. How much of the Scriptures are prophetic? How do you know?

5. What is the role of the Holy Spirit in prophecy?

6. What is the theological meaning of the term inspiration? How does it differ from the way in which we might use this word in everyday speech?

7. What is the theological meaning of the term illumination? What is the relationship between illumination and inspiration?

The Prophetic Work of the Holy Spirit

Segment 2: The Spirit Who Convicts Us of Our Sinfulness

Rev. Terry G. Cornett

In this second segment, we will emphasize that the prophetic Spirit is the one who convicts us of our sinfulness. Every time that the Spirit speaks prophetically, he is seeking to draw us toward the will of God. Therefore, the prophetic work of the Holy Spirit includes not only the revelation of the will of God but also an ongoing ministry in which the Spirit convicts us of disobedience and graciously empowers us to repent of our sins and turn to God. This convicting work of the Holy Spirt is the subject of this segment.

Summary of Segment 2

Our objective for this segment, *The Spirit Who Convicts Us of Our Sinfulness*, is to enable you to:

Rom. 3.9-11
What then? Are we Jews any better off? No, not at all. For we have already charged that all, both Jews and Greeks, are under the power of sin, as it is written: "None is righteous, no, not one; no one understands; no one seeks for God."

- Recognize that human beings are deceived about their sinful condition (its seriousness and consequences) and unwilling and unable to truly seek God and his righteousness.

- Explain the meaning of conviction and describe the Spirit's role in bringing people to a knowledge of their sinful condition.

- Define the key Hebrew and Greek words for repentance.

- Describe the kinds of change that accompany true biblical repentance.

- Demonstrate from the Scriptures that repentance is produced by the work of the Holy Spirit.

2

*Video Segment 2
Outline*

The Holy Spirit overcomes the spiritual blindness of the human race: first, through the conviction of sin, by which the Spirit awakens the sinner to the awareness of sin; and, second, through the grace of repentance, by which the Spirit leads a person to godly sorrow for sin which results in confession and change.

I. **The Spirit's Ministry of Conviction**

A. Definition: conviction is an activity of the Spirit that brings an inner awareness of one's guilt before God. It creates a deep certainty that one is sinful and a realization that one deserves punishment for his or her actions. Conviction undermines the sense of self-justification and excuse-making that accompanies human wrong-doing.

It is best expressed by the words of Isaiah the prophet who said, "Woe is me! For I am lost; for I am a man of unclean lips, and I dwell in the midst of a people of unclean lips; for my eyes have seen the King, the LORD of hosts!" (Isa. 6.5).

B. True conviction of sin is never a human phenomena but is always a work of the Spirit of God.

1. The human heart is deceived, wicked, and unable to grasp its need for God (Gen. 3.13; Gen. 6.5; Ps. 14.1-3; Ps. 36.1-2; Isa. 29.13; Jer. 9.6-8; Rom. 3.-18; 2 Cor. 4.3-4; 2 Tim. 3.12-13).

a. Ps. 53.2-3 - God looks down from heaven on the children of man to see if there are any who understand, who seek after God. They have all fallen away; together they have become corrupt; there is none who does good, not even one.

b. Jer. 17.9 - The heart is deceitful above all things, and desperately sick; who can understand it?

Martin Luther rightly said, "the proud have no taste for grace because their sins do not yet taste bitter to them" (**Luther's Works**, *Jaroslav Pelikan, ed. St. Louis: Concordia, 1958, 14:166).*

2. Jesus explicitly sends the Spirit to convict the world of sin, John 16.7-8.

3. Prophetic speech comes from the Holy Spirit and convicts the unbeliever of sin by exposing the heart (1 Cor. 14.24-25; Heb. 4.12).

4. The preaching and teaching of the prophetic word found in the Scriptures is a key means by which the Holy Spirit convicts of sin.

a. Acts 2.37 (cf. Rom. 10.14-17)

b. Acts 8.26-38

c. See also: Matt. 4.17; Rom. 3.20; 1 Cor. 1.21; 2 Tim. 4.2

II. The Holy Spirit's Work in Repentance

A. Two key biblical words for repentance

1. Old Testament

a. The Hebrew word *shubh-* means "to turn back" or "return."

b. Ezek. 14.6 - Therefore say to the house of Israel, "Thus says the Lord GOD: Repent [*shubh*] and turn away from your idols, and turn away your faces from all your abominations."

c. This word tells us that the person who repents experiences a radical change of attitude which causes them to "turn around," to think and act in a completely different way.

2. New Testament

Metanoia denotes a radical change of mind and heart followed by a behavioral reformation of a sinful life, a sorrowing for sin so as to forsake sin altogether.
~ Thomas C. Oden. *Life in the Spirit.* Systematic Theology: Volume Three. p. 86.

a. The Greek word *metanoia* literally means "a change of mind."

b. 2 Pet. 3.9 - The Lord is not slow to fulfill his promise as some count slowness, but is patient toward you, not wishing that any should perish, but that all should reach repentance [*metanoia*].

c. As used in the Scriptures, it is a deep rich word which might be better stated as a change of *purpose.* This change of purpose involves the whole human being.

B. The changes that are involved in true repentance

1. Repentance involves a change of *MIND.*

a. Before repentance our minds thought of God as an enemy and led us to evil deeds, Col. 1.21-22.

b.   "To set the mind on the flesh is death, but to set the mind on the Spirit is life and peace," Rom. 8.6.

c.   We are called to a renewal of mind, Rom. 12.2 (cf. Eph. 4.17-18).

d.   The most visible sign of a changed mind is our *confession* of sin. We recognize and are willing to call sin things that we previously justified or overlooked (Prov. 28.13; 1 John 1.8-9).

2.   Repentance involves a change of *HEART*.

   a.   The biblical word for this change of heart is contrition.

     (1)   Contrition is humble sorrow over sin.

     (2)   The Hebrew word "contrite" [*dâkâ*] literally means "to be broken into pieces" or "crushed."

     (3)   The sacrifices of God are a broken spirit; a broken and contrite [*dâkâ*] heart, O God, you will not despise, Ps. 51.17.

   b.   True contrition:

     (1)   "Trembles" at the Word of the Lord, Isa. 66.2.

     (2)   Expresses physical and verbal signs of humility, Luke 18.13.

     (3)   Is called "godly sorrow," 2 Cor. 7.10.

     (4)   Expresses true emotional sorrow for sin, Joel 2.12; Zech. 12.10-13.1, and calamity, Joel 2.12.

     (5)   We already mentioned a Hebrew word for repentance, *shubh*, which means "to turn back." There is a second Hebrew word for repentance *nâcham* which is also used throughout the Old Testament. It literally means "to sigh deeply." It suggests that you feel badly about what you have done. It is a term associated

with feelings of regret. It is the word used by Job when he said, *"Therefore I despise myself and **repent** in dust and ashes,"* Job 42.6.

c. The most visible outward signs of a changed heart are emotional anguish and brokenness of spirit. The most reliable outward sign of a changed heart is that the contrite person is ***teachable***. They are through with being stubborn, prideful, or resistant to help.

3. Repentance involves a change of WILL.

a. Repentance versus worldly sorrow

God wants more than just worldly sorrow (2 Cor. 7.10), that is, sorrow that is nothing more than guilty feelings or fear of consequences. The Spirit's goal is a reorienting of the person's will toward God so that life-change results. True repentance always produces a determination to change.

b. The Scriptures consistently teach that true repentance always includes a firm resolve to change wrong behaviors.

(1) Righteous, loving actions are what make it evident that a person belongs to God, 1 John 3.10.

(2) Bear fruit in keeping with repentance, Matt. 3.8.

(3) The parable of the gardener with the unproductive fig tree, Luke 13.1-9

c. The "fruits of repentance"

(1) Repentance is, first and foremost, an act of faith.

(a) Acts 26.20

(b) Repentance is an action that occurs because we believe that what God says about us and about our condition is true. Believing what God says causes us to "change our mind" and "turn around." Therefore the changes in behavior which flow from repentance are technically, "the fruits of repentance" rather than repentance itself.

(2) True faith always produces good works.

    (a) James 2.17

    (b) The faith that produces repentance and the change of life that results from this faith are deeply interconnected. To speak about repentance without also speaking about a changed life is like trying to talk about fire without smoke or heat. Although smoke and heat are simply the results of fire, not fire itself, they are still the surest way to know that something is burning. Likewise, seeing the "fruits of repentance" is the surest way to know that a true change of mind about sin has occurred.

d. The person with a changed will has a genuine desire to repair the damage done by past sins, Luke 19.5-9.

e. The fundamental change of will that take place during true repentance is not accomplished by human resolve, but is a direct result of the activity of the Holy Spirit.

(1) The presence of God's Spirit sustains the human spirit in obedience, Ps. 51.11-12.

(2) The Spirit enables a person to put to death the misdeeds of the body, Rom. 8.13.

(3) The Holy Spirit within a person enables them to obey God, Ezek. 36.27.

Repentance, then, is a result of faith. For unless a man believes that to which he was addicted to be sin, he will not abandon it. And he must believe that punishment looms over the transgressor. . . . Otherwise, he will not reform.
~ Clement of Alexandria (c. 195)

From first to last the good news of the Gospel is that repentance and change of life is not accomplished by human effort. It is while we were still sinners that Christ died for us. And it is while we are spiritually blind to our own sinful condition that the Holy Spirit graciously comes to us to convict us of sin and to give us the gift of true repentance and faith.

(4) The illumination given by the Holy Spirit must come to a person *before* they can respond to God in repentance and faith.

(a) The natural person cannot "receive the things of God" without the help of the Holy Spirit, John 15.26; 1 Cor. 2.14.

The second century theologian Clement of Alexandria described the Holy Spirit's work as being like a magnet that draws men toward God.

(b) Throughout his writings, Paul is clear that when he declares God's Word to people, he is not speaking to a neutral audience. Sin has dramatically affected the ability of human beings to see and accept the truth. In Paul's words, they have a veil over their hearts (2 Cor. 3.14-15), they have been blinded by the god of this world (2 Cor. 4.4), they have ears that will not ear (Rom. 11.8), they are being held in slavery by sin (Rom. 3.9, Rom. 6.17; Eph. 5.8), and they are captives of the spiritual powers that rule the dominion of darkness (Eph. 6.12, Col. 1.13). For Paul, it is foolish to believe that just because the truth has been spoken, people will be able to hear, understand, and believe it. Repentance can only come through the work of the Holy Spirit.

(c) No one can truly say "Jesus is Lord" apart from the work of the Holy Spirit, 1 Cor. 12.3.

[Repentance] is in a very real sense a moral miracle, a gift of grace.
~ Roy Kearsley. *New Dictionary of Theology*. p. 581.

(d) Repentance is a gracious gift, not a consequence of human effort.

One further word about repentance: it is a gift from God. . . . Repentance, accordingly is not doing penance by which we may hope to receive a relationship with God. We may be forever grateful that such is not the case, for we could never be sure that we had done enough. Repentance, rather stems from God's gracious deed in Jesus Christ, whereby our eyes are enlightened, our hearts convicted, and our wills enabled to turn away from sin and bondage to eternal life and liberty. Thanks be unto God!

~ J. Rodman Williams. **Renewal Theology**, Vol. 2. p. 49.

Conclusion

» The Holy Spirit brings people to an awareness of their need for Christ through his ministry of conviction.

» Repentance is a gracious act of God through his Spirit, not a simple act of human effort. No human being seeks, believes, understands, and accepts the Word of God apart from the active ministry of the Holy Spirit.

» True repentance involves a turning from sin and a change of purpose resulting in a changed mind, heart, and will.

The following questions were designed to help you review the material in the second video segment. It is difficult for people to accept that their sinfulness makes it impossible for them to truly seek God, understand his truth, and accept his salvation on their own initiative. Christian leaders need to be clear that only the Spirit of God can show a person their true condition and draw them to Christ. Conviction and repentance does not spring from an act of human determination but from the gracious ministry of the Holy Spirit. Be clear and concise in your answers, and where possible, support with Scripture!

Segue 2

Student Questions and Response

1. What scriptural evidence do we have that people are unable to repent and seek God apart from the drawing of the Holy Spirit?

2. What does it mean to experience conviction of sin? What is the role of the Holy Spirit in conviction?

3. What does the Hebrew word *shubh* mean? What does the Hebrew word *nâcham* mean? What does the Greek word *metanoia* mean? How do each of these words help us more fully understand the biblical meaning of repentance?

4. Repentance involves a turning of the whole human personality to God. What does repentance mean in regards to the mind, the heart, and the will?

5. What are some evidences that a person has truly repented?

6. What is the difference between "godly sorrow" and "worldly sorrow"?

7. What is the relationship between "repentance" and the "fruits of repentance"?

Summary of Key Concepts

This lesson focuses upon the way in which the prophetic work of the Holy Spirit enables us to know and respond to the truth. The Spirit both gives us the truth about God in human words and then empowers us to understand and accept those words. Without the prophetic ministry of the Holy Spirit, no one could know God or understand how to be reconciled to him through his Son.

☞ The knowledge of God cannot come from human effort but only from God's determination to make himself known to us. God reveals himself and his purposes to us through prophetic words inspired by his Holy Spirit.

☞ The Scriptures are the ultimate authority for evaluating claims about God and truth. The Holy Spirit inspired the Scriptures, carrying along the writers so that the words they wrote revealed God's truth. No author of Scripture invented the truths they wrote about, rather they learned them through prophetic revelation. All Scripture is prophecy in this most basic sense.

☞ Prophetic revelation comes through the direct ministry of the Holy Spirit. The prophet is a person whom the Holy Spirit rests upon and prophetic revelation is a gift from the Spirit.

☞ Any claim to prophetic guidance today must be judged and evaluated in light of the Scriptures which are the binding standard of truth for all people, at all times, and in all places.

☞ The Spirit actively illumines (makes clear the meaning) the Scriptures which he inspired. The Spirit illumines the Scriptures both through the ministry of teaching he has given to his Church and through his inner work in the mind and heart of people who hear God's Word.

☞ The Holy Spirit is the means by which God draws people to himself. No human being seeks, believes, understands, and accepts the Word of God apart from the active ministry of the Holy Spirit in their lives.

☞ Jesus explicitly said that it is the job of the Holy Spirit to convict the world of sin. The ministry of the Holy Spirit enables a person to recognize that they are a sinner, guilty before God and deserving of punishment. The convicting ministry of the Holy Spirit strips away excuses and self-justification, produces a revulsion toward sin and genuine remorse over disobedience to God.

CONNECTION

2

↪ Repentance is an act of faith which is produced by the ministry of the Holy Spirit. Repentance involves a complete change of the mind, heart, and will toward one's past way of life. The fruit of repentance is a changed life that devotes itself to God.

Student Application and Implications

Now is the time for you to discuss with your fellow students your questions about *The Prophetic Work of the Holy Spirit*. What particular questions do you have in light of the material you have just studied? Maybe some of the questions below might help you form your own, more specific and critical questions.

* What is the relationship between human reason and human experience and the knowledge of God that comes through inspired revelation?

* Is prophecy a gift available for Christians today? How does the Holy Spirit act as a living voice in the Church? How do we evaluate whether a word of guidance is true?

* How would a Christian leader help a person recognize the difference between "godly sorrow" and "worldly sorrow"?

* Biblical evangelism is centered around a call to "repent and believe the good news" about Jesus. Is God's command that "all people everywhere should repent" (Acts 17.30) adequately expressed and explained in our evangelistic methods and discipleship training?

CASE STUDIES

The Nature Lover

You recently invited Devon, a friend from work, to attend church with you. He said, "I'm not really the church-going type." I believe that we see God better when we are out in his world. Most Sunday mornings I just take a walk in the park. I think I know God better from looking at nature than most people do from hearing a sermon." How do you answer Devon?

Selling Soap and Selling Jesus

Most modern people are saturated with marketing. We hear or see hundreds of commercial advertisements every day. Recently your pastor asked you to be in charge of an evangelistic campaign that would try and tell every person in a ten-block area around your church about Jesus. As you begin to plan for the outreach, you started thinking about the truth that only the Holy Spirit can convince a person of their sin and only the Holy Spirit can give the grace of repentance and faith in Christ. You know it is right to get the "good news" about Jesus out to every person, but you don't want your outreach efforts to act like evangelism is just a "spiritual" form of commercial advertising. What principles will guide you as you plan the outreach? How will you take seriously that only the Holy Spirit can draw people to Christ? Are there some things you must do during the outreach? Are there any things you should not do?

Apology Accepted?

 You are the pastor of a church. One of your parishioners, Rhonda, comes to you in tears. She recently discovered that her husband, Willie, has been having an affair. This was the third time in their nine-year marriage that this has happened. Rhonda says, "Pastor, he says that he is sorry but I'm not sure what that means. I think he is mainly sorry that he got caught. Will you talk to him and tell me what you think?" When you meet with Willie he is congenial and polite. He admits that he did the wrong thing but says "I told her I was sorry but I can't change what I did. She claims to be a Christian, so if she can't accept my apology, it seems like it is more her problem than mine." How will you explain to Willie what true repentance is and how will you evaluate his response to your exhortation?

Restatement of the Lesson's Thesis

The Holy Spirit is the one "who spoke by the prophets." Christians rely on the prophetic word (the Scriptures) given by the Holy Spirit to reveal to them the truth about God. Apart from the inspiration and illumination of the Holy Spirit, there would be no way to truly know what God is like, to understand his will, or to respond to his commands. It is the role of the Holy Spirit to reveal the Father and the Son to us and to draw us toward reconciliation with God.

2

If you are interested in pursuing some of the ideas of *The Prophetic Work of the Holy Spirit*, you might want to give these books a try:

> Thomas C. Oden. Chapter 3, "The Way of Repentance." *Life in the Spirit. Systematic Theology: Vol. Three*. San Francisco: HarperSanFrancisco, 1992.

> Robert L. Saucy. *The Bible: Breathed from God*. The Victor Know and Believe Series. Bruce L. Shelly, ed. Wheaton, IL: Victor Books, 1978.

Resources and Bibliographies

The Apostle James exhorts us to not just listen to the Word, but to obey it. He says that we are blessed, not when we hear the truth, but when we act on it (James 1.22-25). Now is the time to reflect on the implications of this teaching for the actual ministry that God has called you to. How do the doctrines of inspiration and illumination relate to the jobs that God has given you? Who needs to know about the truths you learned concerning conviction and repentance? What particular situation comes to mind when you think about the Holy Spirit's role in drawing people to God and to his truth? Ask the Holy Spirit to help you understand, not only the central truths of this lesson, but also the applications of the truth that he wants to make to your life and ministry. Be specific. Ask the Spirit whether there is an application of this lesson that should be made this very week and then stay alert for the opportunities that he brings you in the coming days. We serve a living God and his Holy Spirit will bring to remembrance everything that we have learned at just the time we need it.

Ministry Connections

Probably everyone in this class is already praying for someone they know who needs to repent and believe the Gospel. It is possible that you yourself are engaged in a struggle with a "sin that easily entangles" (Heb. 12.1). It is vitally important that we remind ourselves that the gracious ministry of the Holy Spirit exists to deal with situations just like these. God worked (and is working) on behalf of people "while they were still sinners" (Rom. 5.8). Find a partner who can pray with you that God would grant repentance to loved ones who do not know Jesus. Pray that the Spirit would convict you, and those in your care, of any sinful action that is displeasing to God and that he would grant true repentance and change of life to everyone involved. We serve a gracious God who is more willing to extend mercy and help than we are to ask for it. The Spirit indwells each one of us who belongs to Christ. Let's ask him to do in us "more than we could ask or imagine" (Eph. 3.20) through the power at work within us.

Counseling and Prayer

2

ASSIGNMENTS

Scripture Memory

Romans 8.18-21

Reading Assignment

To prepare for class, please visit *www.tumi.org/books* to find next week's reading assignment, or ask your mentor.

Other Assignments

Please read carefully the assignments above, and as last week, write a brief summary for them and bring these summaries to class next week (please see the "Reading Completion Sheet" at the end of this lesson). Also, now is the time to begin to think about the character of your ministry project, as well as decide what passage of Scripture you will select for your exegetical project. Do not delay in determining either your ministry or exegetical project. The sooner you select, the more time you will have to prepare!

Looking Forward to the Next Lesson

Our next study, lesson three of our *God the Holy Spirit* module is entitled, *The Powerful Presence of the Holy Spirit*. In this lesson we will begin examining the role that the Spirit plays in the life of the Christian. In particular, we will focus on the way in which the Spirit regenerates us and adopt us into God's family. We will also explore what it means to be "baptized in the Holy Spirit," including some of the ways in which different Christian traditions interpret this biblical concept.

2

Name _____

Date _____

For each assigned reading, write a brief summary (one or two paragraphs) of the author's main point. (For additional readings, use the back of this sheet.)

Reading 1

Title and Author: _____ Pages _____

Reading 2

Title and Author: _____ Pages _____

LESSON
3

The Powerful Presence of the Holy Spirit
Part One

Lesson Objectives

* An acrostic is a word formed by the initial letters of other words or phrases and is used as a way to make ideas easy to memorize. One example of a popular acrostic used in evangelical churches is the word JOY, explained like this: JOY comes when you put Jesus first, Others second, and Yourself last.

Welcome in the strong name of Jesus Christ! After your reading, study, discussion, and application of the materials in this lesson, you will be able to:

- Use the acrostic* "RABBIS" to remember the work of the Holy Spirit in the lives of believers.

- Explain the meaning and theological significance of the Spirit's role in the regeneration, adoption, and baptism of believers in Christ.

- Understand agreements and differences among Christians over the meaning of "baptism in the Holy Spirit."

- Use the Scriptures to show that the work of the Holy Spirit is the means by which God regenerates, adopts, and baptizes those who place their faith in Christ Jesus.

3

Devotion

Jesus the Baptizer

Read Matthew 3.1-12. Christians greatly respect John the Baptist (or John the Baptizer) since he is the forerunner of Jesus, and the last and greatest of the Old Testament prophets. But notice that when John the Baptist preached, he spoke about Jesus the Baptizer. John taught that his own baptism was one of repentance (that is, it would help people show that they were sorry for their sins and that they desired change) but the baptism that Jesus brought would be "mightier" than this. That baptism would not be with water only but with the presence of the Holy Spirit of God. Like fire that burns up chaff, the Holy Spirit would bring not only sorrow for sin but also the destruction of sin. Notice carefully the symbol that Jesus chose to describe this baptism. He said that it would be a baptism of fire. Water only purifies the surface of an object, fire goes all the way through and purifies in a permanent and lasting way. In other words, Jesus baptizes us in the Holy Spirit as a way of making us brand new. The preaching of John the Baptist reminds us that, from the very beginning Jesus came, not only to die for our sins, but also to make it possible for us to receive the Holy Spirit. Thank God, that he sent us not only John the Baptizer, but also Jesus the Baptizer, in order that we might experience the precious and powerful gift of his purifying Holy Spirit.

After reciting and/or singing the Nicene Creed (located in the Appendix), pray the following prayer:

Come, Holy Ghost, our souls inspire, and light us with celestial fire. Amen.

~ Rhabanus Maurus
(German Benedictine monk and theological educator who was
distinguished for his charity to the poor. He lived from 776 to 856 AD).

Nicene Creed and Prayer

. . . .

Put away your notes, gather up your thoughts and reflections, and take the quiz for Lesson 2, *The Prophetic Work of the Holy Spirit.*

Quiz

. . . .

Review with a partner, write out and/or recite the text for last class session's assigned memory verse: Romans 8.18-21.

Scripture Memorization Review

. . . .

Turn in your summary of the reading assignment for last week, that is, your brief response and explanation of the main points that the authors were seeking to make in the assigned reading (Reading Completion Sheet).

Assignments Due

. . . .

3

CONTACT

Behold! I Am Making Everything New!

One of the most widely used words in advertising is the word NEW. Can you name some examples of commercials or products that use this word to sell merchandise? Why is this such an appealing and powerful word? The Scriptures teach the ironic truth that our God, who is known as the "Ancient of Days" (Dan. 7.9), is constantly involved in newness, renewal, and new things. And this is especially true of the works attributed to God the Holy Spirit. In fact the whole Christian life can be described as being made new by the Spirit so that we can live lives full of newness in Christ. As Paul says in Romans 7.6, "But now we are released from the law, having died to that which held us captive, so that we serve not under the old written code but in the new life of the Spirit." How have you personally experienced the newness of life that the Spirit brings?

1

What Does it Mean to Know Someone?

2 If someone said that they knew you well, how would they describe you? (Make a short list of some things they might say). As you look at your list, how many of these things describe who you are (for example, cheerful, patient, friendly, Asian, male, etc.) and how many of these describe what you do (for example, fixes cars, plays basketball, works at Wal-Mart, watches lots of movies)? How do these two different kinds of description give insight into who you really are?

In theology, we describe God in two ways: *his person* (who he is, meaning his character, virtues, and attributes) and *his work* (what he does). When we talk about the person and work of God the Holy Spirit, each of these tells us something important about him. In the next two lessons, we will be concentrating on knowing about the work of the Holy Spirit. Knowing what he does tells us something important about who he is. As we prepare to start this lesson, make a quick list that describes as many works of the Holy Spirit as you can think of in one minute.

Baptism in the Holy Spirit

3 The Spirit of God is the one who draws all believers everywhere into unity. The Apostle Paul, in fact, tells us to "maintain the unity of the Spirit in the bond of peace" (Eph. 4.3). But mention the "baptism in the Holy Spirit" and Christians very often start fighting with each other over what it means, when it occurs, and what shows that it has happened to a person. Given your own tradition, experience, and reading of the Scriptures, how would you answer the question, "What is the 'baptism in the Holy Spirit'?" and "Has it been easy to work together with Christian brothers and sisters who have a different definition from yours? Why or why not?"

3

The Powerful Presence of the Holy Spirit (Part One)

Segment 1: The Spirit Who Regenerates and Adopts

Rev. Terry G. Cornett

CONTENT

The objective of this segment is to show how the Holy Spirit brings God's salvation to us by making us brand new people and placing us into the family of God. After hearing this segment we should understand that:

Summary of Segment 1

- The Holy Spirit is the means by which God transforms us at conversion.

- Because of the "regenerating" work of the Holy Spirit in salvation, we are changed into new people with a new capacity to hear and obey God.

- The Holy Spirit is the way that God comes near to us at conversion, adopting us into God's family, and causing us to understand that God is our loving Father.

- The Holy Spirit baptizes us into Christ Jesus, uniting us to him in his death and resurrection.

3

I. The RABBIS Acrostic

Video Segment 1 Outline

The word *RABBIS* (plural for Jewish Rabbi) will serve as a memory aid for the work of the Holy Spirit in our lives.

A. In the Jewish tradition, a rabbi was someone authorized to teach the Scriptures and explain how people should apply them in their lives. In the same way the Holy Spirit is our divine teacher and counselor who both reveals God's truth to us and also makes clear to us how we can live lives that please God.

B. In this acrostic, each letter of the word RABBIS stands for a specific work of the Holy Spirit in our lives. The work of the Holy Spirit includes:

1. Regeneration

2. Adoption

3. Baptism

4. Bestowing Gifts

5. Indwelling

6. Sealing and Sanctifying

II. The Holy Spirit Regenerates Us.

3

A. The theological term *regeneration*:

    1. Comes from the Greek word *palingenesia*

    2. Means to "birth again" or "make new"

    3. Is used to described a complete change in every part of our being.

B. Regeneration happens when we are converted (saved through faith in Christ Jesus).

1. At conversion we experience both justification and regeneration.

   a. Justification means that we are forgiven by God.

   b. Regeneration means that we are changed by God.

   c. Justification forgives us for being unrighteous while regeneration makes it possible for us to become righteous.

2. The Old Testament anticipates this doctrine of regeneration in passages that speak about God "giving a new heart" (Jer. 24.7; Ezek. 11.19) and "making 'dry bones' live," Ezek. 37.1-14.

3. The New Testament states plainly that it is a work of the Holy Spirit to make us into brand new people.

Titus 3.4-6 - But when the goodness and loving kindness of God our Savior appeared, [5] he saved us, not because of works done by us in righteousness, but according to his own mercy, by the washing of regeneration and renewal of the Holy Spirit, [6] whom he poured out on us richly through Jesus Christ our Savior (see John 3.5-6).

4. There are a series of terms used in Scripture to describe this one experience of regeneration. It is called:

   a. Born anew, John 3.7

   b. Born of God, John 1.13

Regeneration is primarily a work of the Holy Spirit. We have already noted that Jesus said, "That which is born of the flesh is flesh, and that which is born of the Spirit is spirit." Hence, the second birth is by the Holy Spirit.
~ J. Rodman Williams. Renewal Theology. Vol. Two. Grand Rapids: Zondervan, 1990. p. 37.

c. Born of the Spirit, John 3.5

    d. Renewed by the Holy Spirit, Titus 3.5

    e. Passing from death to life, Eph. 1.1,10

    f. Made alive, Eph. 2.5

    g. New creation, Gal. 6.15

    h. New person, Eph. 4.24

    i. Renewal in knowledge in the image of the Creator

       (1) Eph. 4.23-24

       (2) Col. 3.10

    j. All of these describe the Spirit's one work of regeneration that occurs when we place our faith in Christ and are converted.

C. The key theological principles that the Bible teaches about regeneration

    1. *Regeneration is a gift of God that cannot be earned but only received by faith.*

       a. The analogy of birth: no one can choose to be born or pass a test that qualifies them for existence. Life comes to us as a gift and is based on the actions of our parents, not ourselves. In the same way, regeneration can only occur because God chooses to act and it can only be received as a gift (see John 1.12-13, John 3.3-8).

b. The analogy of creation: just as the breath of God entered into Adam and made him into a living person, so at conversion the Spirit of God breathes again into Adam's descendants and restores life to them (2 Cor. 5.17; Gal. 6.15). Human beings are no more responsible for their spiritual creation than they are for their physical creation.

c. Key Verse: Titus 3.4-6

2. *The Word and the Spirit work together to accomplish regeneration.*

a. The Word of God (that is first of all, Jesus Christ, and also, the Gospel that testifies to him) can be said to be the source of regeneration just as the Spirit of God is the source of regeneration.

b. This is one of the great truths that the Protestant Reformation emphasized concerning the Spirit. We can *distinguish* the work of the Spirit in salvation but we cannot *separate* it from the work of the divine Word.

c. Key verses:

(1) 1 Pet. 1.23

(2) James 1.18

(3) John 3.5-6

3. *Regeneration makes us alive but it does not automatically make us mature.*

   a. The image of birth suggests that conversion will need to be followed by steady growth toward maturity. Just as we are not born fully mature, so we are not reborn fully mature (1 Pet. 2.2). While we are sanctified (set apart for God) at conversion, we must grow up into Christ (Eph. 4.15, 2 Pet. 3.18).

   b. Key verse: 1 Pet. 2.2

4. *The regeneration of individuals is part of a larger work of the Spirit to regenerate all things.*

   a. God's plan of salvation in not just to save people from death but to set right everything that has been harmed, corrupted and destroyed. God is saving our planet and our universe and our salvation is a part of that much larger process.

   b. Matt. 19.28 - "I tell you the truth, *at the renewal* [*palingenesia* = regeneration] *of all things*" (cf. Acts 3.19-21; Rom. 8.19-24).

   c. This regeneration of all things (that is, the entire created order) is prophesied in both the Old Testament and the New (see, for example, Isaiah 11.6-9 and Revelation 21.1-5).

   d. This future regeneration of all things is an extension of the current work of the Holy Spirit who constantly preserves and renews all creation (Ps. 104.27-30).

3

III. The Holy Spirit Adopts Us

In the Roman world, adoption was "the process by which a person was transferred from his natural father's power into that of his adoptive father; and it consisted in a fictitious sale of the son, and his surrender by the natural to the adoptive father" (*International Standard Bible Encyclopedia*, Vol. One, p. 54).

A. Why we need to be adopted by God

1. Following Adam's sin, all human beings came under the authority of evil (1 John 3.8). In one passage, Jesus even speaks about those who have not accepted him as having the devil for their father (John 8.44). This is why the Bible speaks about conversion as a change in authority from darkness to light, or from being under the power of the devil to coming under the power of God.

2. Since we are by nature "children of wrath" (Eph. 2.3), we cannot claim a natural place in the family of God. Instead, we must be brought into his family through adoption.

B. Adoption is a work of the Holy Spirit.

1. Rom. 8.14-17

2. Eph. 2.18-19 (cf. Rom. 8.9)

Rom. 9.26
And in the very place where it was said to them, "You are not my people," there they will be called "sons of the living God."

Paul's argument for Gentile salvation is based on an implicit adoption argument. They were not actually God's people but rather must be brought into kinship relationship by a deliberate decision of God.

C. The key theological principles that the Bible teaches about adoption

    1. *God is the Creator of all people but not the Father of all.*

        a. 1 John 3.8 (cf. John 8.44)

        b. No human being naturally belongs to God's family. We are not born into God's family as infants but rather must become adopted children of God (Eph. 1.5) through faith in Christ Jesus.

        c. Key verse: Gal. 3.26

    2. *Becoming a child of God is not a right but a privilege.*

        a. We have no claim on God or his love (Matt. 3.9; Rom. 3.10-12; Eph. 2.3).

        b. God's gracious love is the only reason he adopts us. (Rom. 4.16; Rom. 5.20-21; Eph. 2.8-9; Titus 3.4-5).

        c. Key verses:

          (1) Eph. 2.3-5

          (2) 1 John 3.1

Ministry Insight

Adoption helps us understand that we are not in control of our salvation. (You can pick your friends but not your family). New converts are not simply coming to Jesus, they are coming to the family of God.

3

3. *Adoption reminds us that salvation always involves becoming a part of God's Church.* Salvation literally involves being placed in a new family which we call the Church.

   a. God's adoption of us results in a change of family identity. The Apostle Paul writes that the Church is, in fact, the very household of God (1 Tim. 3.15; Eph. 2.19-20).

   b. Adopted children naturally desire to be in their Father's house with their brothers and sisters (Acts 2.42; Heb. 2.11-13; 10.25).

   c. Key verse: Eph. 2.19-20

4. *Adoption gives intimate access to God* – becoming a member of God's family gives a person both rights and responsibilities.

   a. Through adoption we gain the right to call God "Abba" (Mark 14.36; Rom. 8.14-17; Rom. 8.29) which is an intimate personal term like "daddy" or "papa" in English.

   b. As adopted children, God reveals himself and his plans in a unique way to us, his family (1 Cor. 2.12-13; Rom. 8.32).

   c. God's discipline demonstrates our adopted standing as full sons and daughters (see Heb. 12.5-11).

   d. Key verse: Rom. 8.14-18

Ministry Insight

It makes a difference to belong to the Church. New converts must be taught to treasure time spent with the family. Belonging to the Church is quantitatively different from belonging to any other institution.

Ministry Insight
Once you have said yes to the lordship of Christ the Holy Spirit will no longer ask for permission to interfere in your life. One of the great joys of being a Christian is that you no longer get left alone. Just as with our natural parents, God our Father no longer leaves us to do whatever we want. Parents do not need permission to intervene in our lives. Most of us know what it is like to have parents that looked out for us, that guided us, and that disciplined us, whether we wanted them to or not. Adoption into God's family creates that same intimate relationship with our heavenly Father.

The Old Testament story of Jonah captures some of this meaning of being someone who belongs to God. The following poem has always captured for me this sense of the Spirit's work in Jonah's life and in our own.

The Great Intruder

*It is exasperating
to be called
so persistently
when the last thing
we want to do
is get up
and go
but God
elects
to keep on haunting
like some
holy ghost.*

~ Thomas John Carlisle. **You! Jonah!**
Grand Rapids, MI: Eerdmans, 1968.

5. *Adoption places a person in line for an inheritance from God.*

    a. Matt. 25.34

    b. As members of God's family we are inheriting the Kingdom of God (Matt. 25.34; Col. 1.12-13; Eph. 1.13-14;1 Pet. 1.3-4).

    c. Key verse: Col. 1.12-13

Conclusion

» At conversion, the Holy Spirit regenerates us (makes us new people) so that we both want to obey God and have the power to do so.

» At conversion, the Holy Spirit adopts us into God's family so that can we experience his constant presence with us, be treated as God's sons and daughters, and be joined to God's household which is the Church.

The questions below are designed to help you identify the key points in our last video segment on "The Spirit Who Regenerates and Adopts." Please answer the following questions carefully, be clear and concise in your answers, and where possible, support with Scripture!

1. What does the word "regeneration" mean?

2. What is the difference between justification and regeneration?

3. What are some of the other terms used in Scripture to define the experience of regeneration?

4. What is the relationship between the work of the Son of God and the work of the Spirit of God in bringing regeneration to a person?

5. Besides individual people, what else does the Bible teach that God will regenerate?

6. Why is the doctrine of adoption necessary?

7. What evidences would show that a person has received "the Spirit of adoption?"

8. What rights and responsibilities come with being adopted into the family of God?

9. Given the strong association of regeneration with "new life" and "new birth," what things do churches need to do to nurture and protect those who are new Christians?

Segue 1

Student Questions and Response

3

The Powerful Presence of the Holy Spirit (Part One)

Segment 2: The Baptism in the Holy Spirit

Rev. Terry G. Cornett

Summary of Segment 2

In the first segment we sought to show how the Spirit is the one who enables us to be spiritually reborn and placed into the family of God, through regeneration and adoption. In this second segment, we will speak about the biblical image of being "baptized into the Spirit of God" and the role that the Spirit plays in connecting believers to Christ and empowering them to minister in his name.

Our objective for this segment, *The Baptism in the Holy Spirit,* is to:

- Remind students that the baptism of the Holy Spirit is an important scriptural doctrine.

- Explain some key elements of the Spirit's work in uniting us to Christ.

- Help students understand that Christians disagree about Spirit baptism including what it accomplishes, and when and how it happens.

- Allow students to summarize the major views about Spirit baptism and see how each is defended from the Scriptures.

- Help students to understand and defend their own position on Spirit baptism as well as understand and learn from the views of others.

We will continue to use the RABBIS acrostic to understand the ministry of the Holy Spirit as we discuss the first "B"– baptism in the Holy Spirit.

Video Segment 2 Outline

I. Introduction

A. This is a theological topic over which the Church genuinely disagrees! There is no way to completely resolve the disagreement and we should not pretend otherwise. However, there is some common ground that can be found in the midst of the disagreements.

B.   Common ground: joined to Christ and his Church through the ministry of the Spirit

1.   The Scriptures teach us that we receive the Holy Spirit at the moment of salvation and that he joins us to Christ and his Church in such a way that we not only have the right to be there (as adoption makes clear) but also that we experience the living power and presence of Christ and his people because we share the Holy Spirit with them.

2.   1 Cor. 12.13

3.   NOTE: Although not every theological tradition would necessarily refer to this aspect of the Spirit's work as "the baptism in the Holy Spirit" (some would prefer to call it being "born of the Spirit"), all would agree that a major work of the Holy Spirit is to unite us to Jesus and his body and to be the living power and presence of Christ in our lives. Regardless of what we call it, this is a key area of Christian agreement.

C.   Areas of disagreement about Spirit baptism: the key questions

For many Christians the above definition (union with Christ and his Church) means that being "baptized in the Holy Spirit" is something that happens to all Christians at the moment of conversion. However, many Christians think that certain Bible verses might raise other questions about Spirit baptism. They ask: "Do we receive all that the Holy Spirit has for us at the moment of salvation or is there a greater fullness of the Holy Spirit that comes later in our Christian experience?" "If so, how is this fullness received, what evidences show that it has happened, and what might it accomplish?"

* These are things that Christians agree are done by and through the Holy Spirit even in those traditions that reserve the term "baptism in the Holy Spirit" for another aspect of the Spirit's work.

II. The Baptism in the Holy Spirit: Areas of General Agreement*

A. We receive the Holy Spirit at the moment of salvation (Rom. 8.9; 1 Cor. 12.13).

B. Spirit baptism is a joint work of God the Father, Jesus Christ, and the Holy Spirit, Matt. 3.11.

C. We are baptized (*baptizo* - to be immersed or submerged) in the Holy Spirit so that the Spirit can do his work of connecting us to Christ and his Church.

   1. Spirit baptism connects us to Christ and others.

      a. 1 Cor. 12.13

      b. 2 Cor. 13.14

      c. The word fellowship is from the Greek word *koinonia* which can also be translated communion. It is the activity that makes community, that connects and unites people who share a common bond.

   2. The connecting element of Spirit baptism was anticipated in the Hebrew Scriptures, Isa. 44.3-5.

   3. The connecting element of Spirit baptism is confirmed in the New Testament Scriptures.

a. The gift of the Holy Spirit caused the Church to be born, Acts 2.38-39.

b. The gift of the Holy Spirit connects us to Christ and his Church (1 Cor. 12.13; Eph. 4.4-6).

....

In Paul the gift of the Spirit is the beginning of Christian experience (Gal. 3.2-3), another way of describing the new relation of justification (1 Cor. 6.11; Gal. 3.14; Titus 3.7). Alternatively expressed, one cannot belong to Christ unless one has the Spirit of Christ (Rom. 8.9), one cannot be united with Christ except through the Spirit (1 Cor. 6.17), one cannot share Christ's sonship without sharing his Spirit (Rom. 8.14–17; Gal. 4.6-7), one cannot be a member of the body of Christ except by being baptized in the Spirit(1 Cor. 12.13).

~ J. D. G. Dunn. **New Bible Dictionary**. p. 1139.

....

c. The key theological principles defended from Scripture

(1) *Through the baptism in the Spirit, we are united with Christ.*

(a) Rom. 8.9

(b) John 7.37-39

(c) 1 Cor. 6.17

(d) No one can claim to know Christ if they have not experienced this living connection with him through the outpouring of the Holy Spirit. The result of this baptism in the Spirit is that we are now referred to as "in Christ" (see Rom. 8.1;16.7; 2 Cor. 5.17; Eph. 2.6-7; Col. 2.9-10; 1 Pet. 5.14).

(e) Through the Holy Spirit, we are united to Jesus so that his life, his death, his resurrection, and his access to God the Father become our own.

(2) *Through Spirit baptism we are incorporated into the Church.*

    (a) 1 Cor. 12.13

    (b) Eph. 2.19-22

    (c) 1 Cor. 3.16-17, Do you not know that you are God's temple and that God's Spirit dwells in you? [17] If anyone destroys God's temple, God will destroy him. For God's temple is holy, and you are that temple. {Note- the word "you" is plural in the Greek. The meaning is "all of you" are God's temple}.

III. The Baptism in the Holy Spirit: Understanding the Areas of Disagreement

A. Two different ways of understanding how the Holy Spirit comes to us

1. *The single-stage view* of Spirit baptism believes that all of the person and work of the Holy Spirit is received at the moment of salvation and that the rest of the Christian life is an outworking (or a growing up into) what was received at that moment. In this view, the work of the Holy Spirit in a person's life after salvation is primarily gradual and progressive.

2. *Multiple-stage views* of Spirit baptism are those which believe the Holy Spirit is received in two or more stages and which include a distinct experience after salvation which imparts "the fullness of the Spirit." In other words, while the person of the Holy Spirit is received at salvation, there are specific works of the Holy Spirit that are received later. In these theologies, the term "baptism in the Holy Spirit" is often reserved for the experiences (the specific works of empowerment for ministry or victory over sin) that come later rather than to describe the initial coming of the person of the Spirit at salvation.

3

3. There are Scriptures that can be cited in support of both the single-stage and multiple-stage views.

   a. The Pauline letters tend to emphasize more strongly the coming of the Holy Spirit at salvation and his work of uniting us to Christ as the key element of Spirit baptism.

   b. Luke's writings (Luke and Acts) tend to emphasize more strongly the work of the Holy Spirit in coming on a person so that they are enabled to minister with power (witness) as the key element of Spirit baptism. This miraculous power often seems to be spoken of as a second-stage of the Spirit's work.

   c. Paul and Luke do not disagree with each other but emphasize differing sides of a common truth. Whether we hold a single-stage view or a multiple-stage view, it is important that we take both Paul and Luke seriously and strive to understand how their views work together to express one common truth about the Holy Spirit.

B. The single-stage view of Spirit baptism

   1. The single-stage view is often called the Reformed view of Spirit baptism. This understanding of Spirit baptism is what you are likely to find in churches with a Presbyterian, Reformed, or Baptist heritage, among others.

   2. Union with Christ is the key to understanding salvation.

      To be united to Christ in his life, death, and resurrection is what distinguishes a Christian from a non-Christian. Because of union with Christ, everything that Christ has God counts as belonging to us.

3. At salvation, (when we are united with Christ), we receive the same access to the Holy Spirit that Jesus has.

    In terms of baptism in the Holy Spirit, this means that since Jesus possesses the Spirit "without limit"(John 3.34-35), that same resource is bestowed on us in Christ. This view would argue that you cannot have more of the Holy Spirit than you receive at salvation because at salvation you are given access to everything that belongs to Christ.

4. Christian maturity involves learning how to live moment by moment in dependence on the power of the Holy Spirit that God gives us at the moment of salvation.

    a. This view emphasizes that new believers often do not realize what they have been given or know how to live out their new life in the Spirit. At salvation, we are given the Holy Spirit who fully and completely indwells (1 Cor. 6.19) and empowers us, but we must learn to "walk in the Spirit" (Gal. 5.16-26) on a daily basis. For the Reformed position, every believer has been "baptized in the Holy Spirit" but not every believer has matured so that they are walking in the power and holiness that would make that evident. This growth in the Spirit filled life is an on-going process that never stops. Even the most mature believer will not experience complete freedom from sin and complete reliance on the Spirit's power, until they die and are glorified.

    b. Exegetical distinctive: The Reformed view draws the majority of it's theology about baptism in the Holy Spirit from the Pauline Epistles. The Stories of the Book of Acts must be harmonized with the plain propositional statements of Paul.

It would certainly be a mistake to try to base a doctrine of theological necessity upon passages in Luke's writings [Acts] which were designed to describe the various stages which seemed to him significant in the spread of a work for God.
~ Michael Green. *I Believe in the Holy Spirit*. p. 162.

3

5. Summary of the Reformed Position

    a. What is the "baptism in the Holy Spirit"?

        The means by which a person is united to Christ and his Church (1 Cor. 12.7, 13; Eph. 4.4-5; Gal. 3.2).

    b. When is the "fullness of the Holy Spirit" received?

        At conversion when a person repents and believes in Jesus as Savior and Lord (Acts 2.38-39, Rom. 8.9).

    c. How is the "fullness of the Spirit" received?

        By saving faith in Jesus Christ (John 7.37-39)

    d. What is the evidence or confirmation that the "fullness of the Spirit" was received?

        Perseverance in the faith (John 15.4; Phil. 3.12-14)

    e. What does the "fullness of the Holy Spirit" accomplish?

        It makes us more and more like Jesus Christ (2 Cor. 3.18; John 15.4, Rom. 12.1-2).

C. Multiple-stage views of Spirit baptism

    1. Multiple-stage views believe that the Spirit is given at salvation but that a greater fullness of the Spirit is received at a later point in time which enables a person to more completely experience the work of the Spirit in their life and ministry.

2. Those who believe that the Holy Spirit comes upon people in two or more stages have different views about what this accomplishes but they all appeal to the same scriptural evidence to support the main idea that the Holy Spirit does a second work in people following salvation. Here are some of the main Scripture passages that are appealed to.

    a. Philip's mission to Samaria (Acts 8)

        Philip baptizes people as new Christians but they receive the "fulness" of the Holy Spirit only after Peter and John come and lay hands on them.

    b. Paul at the house of Ananias (Acts 9)

        Paul is converted on the road to Damascus and receives his commission to missionary service (see Acts 26.13-19) but is filled with the Holy Spirit only after Ananias lays hands on him.

    c. John the Baptist's disciples are baptized in Jesus' name by Paul (Acts 19).

        Disciples baptized by John the Baptist knew that Jesus was the Messiah but had been inadequately instructed about the Holy Spirit. Paul asks them "Did you receive the Holy Spirit when you believed?" Multiple-stage views suggest that this is not a question that makes any sense unless there is some special experience with the Holy Spirit that is different from conversion itself.

    d. The experience of Jesus' Apostles

        (1) In John 20.22 - Jesus breathes on the apostles and they receive the Holy Spirit but in Acts 1.4-8, he instructs these same apostles to wait in Jerusalem for the coming of the Holy Spirit so that they can receive power to be witnesses.

3

(2) Acts 1.4-5 - And while staying with them he ordered them not to depart from Jerusalem, but to wait for the promise of the Father, which, he said, "you heard from me; [5] for John baptized with water, but you will be baptized with the Holy Spirit not many days from now."

3. The churches that teach that there is a distinct experience with the Holy Spirit following the one that occurs at conversion include: Roman Catholic*, Holiness, and Pentecostal churches. In the following section, we will be examining both the Holiness and the Pentecostal positions.

    a. Baptism in the Holy Spirit: the Holiness View

        (1) Examples of Holiness churches include: the Church of God (Anderson, IN), Church of the Nazarene, the Free Methodist Church, etc.

        (2) Key exegetical assumption: think globally about the whole witness of Scripture rather than starting with a few key texts about the topic and trying to reason exclusively from them.

        (3) "Entire sanctification" (sometimes called Christian perfection) is possible in this life and God expects us to seek hard after it but it is not attainable by mere human effort (it is a gift of grace) and therefore, it must be received from the Holy Spirit and his

....

*Briefly stated, the Roman Catholic view of Spirit baptism is as follows: The Holy Spirit is received at water baptism to join the believer to the Church. This is viewed as the "baptism of the Holy Spirit" promised by Jesus (**Catechism of the Catholic Church**, pp. 190, 312, 321-22). There is no essential distinction between "water baptism" and "spirit baptism."*

*However, in Roman Catholic theology "the sacrament of Confirmation is necessary for the completion of baptismal grace. For by the sacrament of Confirmation, [the baptized] are more perfectly bound to the Church and are enriched with a special strength of the Holy Spirit" (**CCC**, p. 325-26). This experience is understood as increasing the gifts of the Holy Spirit in the believer (**CCC** p. 330). This "fullness of the Spirit" (**CCC** p. 326) is received by the laying of hands, anointing with oil, and an invocation by the bishop (**CCC** p. 329). Therefore, as in Holiness and Pentecostal theologies there is a second-stage experience at which the fulness of the Holy Spirit is received.*

It is critical to remember that Wesleyans do not come to their biblical understanding of sanctification by a system of logical deductions from certain proof texts or propositions. Their convictions on the possibilities of perfection in love in this life and a faith experience of heart cleansing subsequent to justification grow out of their attempt to see Scripture holistically.
~ Melvin Dieter, former provost of Asbury Theological Seminary. Five Views on Sanctification. Grand Rapids: Zondervan-HarperCollins. 1987.

action upon the believer (see Appendix 22 for a further clarification of "entire sanctification" in these churches including scriptural support and its relationship to the baptism in the Holy Spirit).

(4) Sanctification is separate from and must logically follow salvation. While this may be immediate, it often is a number of years before this happens.

(5) The baptism in the Holy Spirit is a second experience following conversion in which the Holy Spirit brings a person into "Christian perfection" or "entire sanctification." It is the means by which a person comes to fully desire, and is empowered to live, a holy life. This means abstaining from willful sin and walking in love for God and for people.

(6) *Summary of the Holiness Position*

   (a) What is the "baptism in the Holy Spirit"?

   A crisis experience in which the Christian is "perfected in love" and empowered to live a holy life. This is often called the "second blessing" or "second work of grace."

   (b) When is the "fullness of the Holy Spirit" received?

   Different for each person but always after justification (conversion)

   (c) How is the "fullness of the Spirit" received?

   Repentance and faith, earnest seeking in prayer

   (d) What is the evidence or confirmation that the "fullness of the Spirit" was received?

   Holiness of life, defined as victory over known sin and love for others

b. Baptism in the Holy Spirit: the Pentecostal view

(1) Exegetical distinctive: using the Book of Acts as the primary source for understanding the baptism in the Holy Spirit (see Keener, "What Can Bible Stories Teach Us?" Appendix, *Holy Spirit: Gift and Giver* for an explanation and defense of this approach). Pentecostals historically relied on Luke's accounts to lay the foundation for their theology and argued that the statements of Paul in the Epistles (which are generally directed toward problem-solving in particular church situations) must be integrated into the more universal narrative of the Gospels and Acts.

(2) Pentecostals believe that there is a difference between indwelling and infilling. Pentecostals often teach that the Spirit indwells a Christian at salvation but fills them up at the time of Spirit baptism.

(3) Some Pentecostals teach that at salvation "the Holy Spirit baptizes us into Christ" (1 Cor. 12.13) but that the baptism in the Spirit, is a separate time when "Christ baptizes us in the Holy Spirit" (Mark 1.8). Therefore, the baptism in the Holy Spirit is an event that happens after conversion and gives power for mission and ministry (cf. Acts 1.4, 8; 8.14-16).

(4) For most Pentecostals, the initial (and necessary) evidence of baptism in the Holy Spirit is speaking in tongues, according to the pattern that they see in the Book of Acts (Acts 2.1-4; 10.45-46; 19.5-6, see also Mark 16.17-18).

(5) *Summary of the Pentecostal position*

(a) What is the "baptism in the Holy Spirit"?

A crisis experience in which the Christian is filled with the power of the Holy Spirit to effectively engage in ministry and mission

(b) When is the "fullness of the Holy Spirit" received?

Different for each person but always after justification (conversion)

(c) How is the "fullness of the Spirit" received?

i) "The only condition for receiving the promise of the Father is repentance and faith" (Stanley M. Horton). However, Pentecostals stress that the faith they are describing is "active, obedient faith" (William Menzies, *Bible Doctrines*, by Menzies and Horton, p. 130).

ii) Earnest seeking in prayer accompanied by an attitude of surrender and willingness to be baptized by Christ into his Spirit, and faith that he will do so. This prayer is normally done in the presence of other believers who lay hands on the seeker and agree in prayer.

(d) What is the evidence or confirmation that the "fullness of the Spirit" was received?

Speaking in tongues is the initial evidence. Spiritual power is the continuing evidence.

(e) What does the "fullness of the Holy Spirit" accomplish?

Gives increased power for ministry, mission, and holy living, including but not limited to, an increased ability to exercise spiritual gifts.

The primary purpose of the baptism is to give greater power for witnessing (Acts 1.8).
~ www.ag.org/top/ beliefs/baptism_hs/ baptmhs_01_distinct.cfm (Assemblies of God website)

c. Baptism in the Holy Spirit: the Pentecostal-Holiness view

(1) There are some churches which combine these views and are known as Pentecostal-Holiness churches. This includes denominations like the Church of God in Christ [5 million USA, 8 million world], Church of God (Cleveland, TN), Apostolic Faith churches, and the Pentecostal Holiness Church.

(2) These churches teach three distinct experiences with the Holy Spirit.

(a) First, salvation where the Holy Spirit unites a person to Christ (what the Reformed view would call baptism in the Holy Spirit).

3

(b) Second, "entire sanctification" where the Spirit frees the believer from willful sin and perfects the believer in love (what the Holiness view would call baptism in the Holy Spirit).

(c) Third, baptism in the Holy Spirit, evidenced by speaking in tongues, where the Spirit endows the believer with power for mission and ministry (same definition as the Pentecostal view).

Conclusion

» Christians agree that the Spirit must, in some way, come upon a person at salvation if they are to be cleansed from sin and united to Christ.

» Some Christians (the Reformed view) believe that the rest of the Christian life is simply progressively learning more and more about the powerful presence of the Holy Spirit that has been given at salvation.

» Other Christians (Holiness and Pentecostal Christians) believe that the Book of Acts teaches that Christian should have further experiences with the Holy Spirit that give powerful new advances in holiness and ministry effectiveness.

» All Christians should agree that learning to depend on the power of the Holy Spirit is the key to becoming God's person and doing his work.

» Theologian J. I. Packer brings the different definitions of Spirit baptism into common agreement when he says, "Since experience of apostolic quality is rare and much to be desired, and the church today is weak for the lack of it, it is right to ask God to lead us into it, by whatever name we call it and in whatever theology we express it" ("Baptism in the Holy Spirit," *New Dictionary of Theology*, p. 74).

Segue 2

Student Questions and Response

These questions are designed to help you review and discuss the truths that were presented concerning the baptism in the Holy Spirit in our last segment "The Powerful Presence of the Holy Spirit (Part One)." Please take as much time as you have available to answer these and other questions that the video brought out. Be clear and concise in your answers, and where possible, support with Scripture!

1. The Scriptures sometimes speak of the baptism in the Holy Spirit primarily in terms of God's presence and, at other times, primarily in terms of God's power. How would you answer a person who said that it was possible to be a Christian but not yet have the presence of the Holy Spirit?

2. How would you explain the single-stage (Reformed) view of Spirit baptism? What Scriptures might help support this view?

3. What Scriptures might support a multiple-stage view of Spirit baptism?

4. How would you explain the Holiness view of Spirit baptism?

5. How would you explain the Pentecostal view of Spirit baptism?

6. How would you explain the Pentecostal-Holiness view of Spirit baptism?

3

Summary of Key Concepts

This lesson focuses on the ways that the Holy Spirit brings us into the body of Christ and prepares us to function as God's people in the world.

↪ Regeneration is the work of the Holy Spirit that causes us to be "born again." Through regeneration, the Holy Spirit changes the inside of a person so that they are no longer controlled by a sinful nature but instead have a brand new spirit inside them that is created in the image of Christ.

↪ Regeneration is a free gift of God that cannot be earned by good works or human effort. Just as life came to us from our parents without us doing anything to earn or deserve it, so regeneration comes as a free gift from God that can only be received by faith.

↪ The regenerating work of the Holy Spirit makes us alive but not mature. Just as human birth is followed by the need for growth toward maturity, so spiritual birth is also followed by the need to grow up in Christ.

- The Holy Spirit's work of regenerating individuals is part of his larger work to make all things new. The Holy Spirit is at work to fulfill God's ultimate plan to create a new heaven and a new earth in which all things are freed from the effects of sin.

- Because of our father Adam's sin, we are by nature "children of wrath" and cannot claim to be God's children by any natural descent. The Holy Spirit adopts believers into God's family at the moment they place their faith in Christ and, completely by grace, gives them the rights and inheritance belonging to royal children. This adoption guarantees us both unique intimacy with God and also discipline and correction when we fail to obey him.

- The Holy Spirit's ministry of adoption reminds us that salvation can never be separated from incorporation into the Church. To accept Christ always involves being adopted into his family (the Church) and thus no one is saved apart from the whole family of God.

- One of the most important works of the Holy Spirit at salvation is his work of uniting us to Christ so that the power of Jesus' life, death, resurrection, and ascension are credited to us and set at work in us. The Reformed tradition emphasizes that this occurs as the Holy Spirit living in us makes the presence of Christ real in our lives and speaks of this work as the baptism in the Holy Spirit following Paul's language about the Spirit who baptizes us into Christ's body.

- Many Protestant Christians who are not in the Reformed tradition prefer to use the term "baptism in the Holy Spirit" to refer to an experience that follows conversion. Rather than connecting Spirit baptism to the Spirit's presence (as the Reformed tradition does), these believers follow Luke in emphasizing Spirit baptism as a special endowment of God's power.

- It is important that we do not mistakenly set Paul's writings against Luke's but accept the entire witness of the Scriptures (Gospels, Acts, and Epistles) and find ways to speak about Spirit baptism which emphasize *both* his presence and his power, *both* his work at salvation and his work following salvation. Christians may disagree about the theological language used for this dependence on the Spirit's presence and power but all should seek to experience it.

Student Application and Implications

Now is the time for you to discuss with your fellow students your questions about the ministry of the Holy Spirit which have been raised by today's lesson. Your questions are of the utmost importance. The ideas, questions, and concerns that you have now must be discussed and debated. The truth regarding the work of the Holy Spirit in this lesson is full of important implications, and undoubtedly you now have questions regarding the significance of these truths for your work in the Church, and for your life and ministry. The following questions may help you form your own, more specific and critical questions.

* What are the implications of the Spirit's regenerating work (which the Scriptures refer to as new birth, making new, making alive, new creation) for people in the city?

* How should the Spirit's work of adopting new believers into God's family affect the way that we think about the Church? What are the strengths that your church has as acting as a family for new believers? Are there any things that should be improved?

* In your church, when and how is the Spirit's work of regeneration and adoption explained to a new believer? What has worked well for you in this process? Are there ways that you can improve this?

* What does your church believe about baptism in the Holy Spirit? Do you hold a single-stage or a multiple-stage view? Why?

* How do we keep our differing views over baptism in the Holy Spirit from becoming something that gives the devil a chance to cause division in the body of Christ or causing one group of Christians to feel more spiritual than another?

How New Is He?

A middle-aged man with a troubled history as a pedophile recently accepted Christ through the outreach ministry of your church. He is attending every service and is eagerly soaking up the Scriptures through group Bible studies and hours of personal reading at home. It is obvious that he has had an encounter with Christ and that rapid change is happening in his life. He has publicly renounced his old way of life and has agreed to meet regularly with an accountability partner (assigned by the senior pastor) who can support him in his struggles with temptation and to whom he can confess any failures. While the people of the church were thrilled when he accepted Christ, and rejoiced with him as he gave his testimony, some of the parents in the church have recently begun to express concerns that he may be a danger to their children. Last Sunday a small group of parents came up to the pastor after church and said that if this man continued to attend the church, they would feel compelled to take their children elsewhere. How should the biblical teaching on the Holy Spirit's work of regeneration and adoption guide the pastor as he talks with the parents and as he provides pastoral care for the new convert and the congregation?

I'm Not Sure What to Think

Janice has been a Christian for about two years. She has been a faithful church attender who has "soaked up" the Bible teaching offered through sermons and Bible studies. Everyone at the church would agree that she is a growing Christian who loves Jesus and wants to serve him faithfully. Recently she was reading the Book of Acts and came across Paul's question to the disciples at Ephesus in Acts 19, "Did you receive the Holy Spirit when you believed?" She comes to you in an obvious state of confusion. She says, "I know that God came into me two years ago and changed me life. I've always assumed that was the work of the Holy Spirit but now I'm not so sure. Did I receive the Holy Spirit when I believed? Is there some other experience with the Holy Spirit that I need to have? I just don't know what to think about all this." What should you tell her? Why?

The Holy Spirit of God is the one who regenerates us (makes us new) and adopts us into God's family. To be baptized (immersed) in the Spirit of God both unites us to Christ and his Church and also gives us access to God's power for holiness and witness. Christians disagree about whether the fulness of the Holy Spirit is received at conversion (Reformed view) or whether a distinct experience with the Holy Spirit to give the believer increased power should occur following conversion (Holiness and Pentecostal views).

Restatement of the Lesson's Thesis

Resources and Bibliographies

If you are interested in reading more regarding the Holy Spirit's work in the life of the Church and the individual believer, you might want to give these books a try:

Fee, Gordon. *Paul, the Spirit, and the People of God*. Peabody, MA: Hendrickson, 1996.

Graham, Billy. *The Holy Spirit: Activating God's Power in Your Life*. Dallas, TX: Word Publishing, 1997.

Green, Michael. *I Believe in the Holy Spirit*. Grand Rapids, MI: Wm. B. Eerdmans, 1975.

Ministry Connections

Seeking to relate these truths to your own ministry through your church represents the core of this teaching. How God might want you to change or alter your ministry approach based on these truths is largely dependent on your ability to hear what the Holy Spirit is saying to you about where you are, where your pastoral leadership is, where the members of your church are, and what specifically God is calling you to do right now, if anything, about these truths. Plan to spend good time this week meditating on the work of the Holy Spirit in the life of the believer. As you consider your ministry project for this module, you can possibly use it to connect to these truths in a practical way. Seek the face of God for insight, and come back next week ready to share your insights with the other learners in your class.

3

Counseling and Prayer

Perhaps there are some specific needs or questions which the Holy Spirit has surfaced through your study and discussion of this material on the Holy Spirit. Do not hesitate to find a partner in prayer who can share the burden and lift up your requests to God. Of course, your instructor is extremely open to walking with you on this, and your church leaders, especially your pastor, may be specially equipped to help you answer any difficult questions arising from your reflection on this study. Be open to God and allow him to lead you as he determines.

Romans 8.22-25

To prepare for class, please visit *www.tumi.org/books* to find next week's reading assignment, or ask your mentor.

As usual you ought to come with your reading assignment sheet containing your summary of the reading material for the week. Also, you should continue to work on your exegetical project, and *turn in your proposal for your ministry project* which is due after the session.

Next session we complete our module on the Holy Spirit by continuing to focus on the work that the Holy Spirit does in the life of the believer. Praise God for the promise of Christ that he would not leave us alone but would send the Holy Spirit to be his own living presence in our lives (John 14.18). The key to living the Christian life is understanding that we have not been left to our own effort and wisdom but rather that, through the Holy Spirit, the power and presence of Christ is constantly with his people.

3

For each assigned reading, write a brief summary (one or two paragraphs) of the author's main point. (For additional readings, use the back of this sheet.)

Reading 1

Title and Author: _____ Pages _____

Reading 2

Title and Author: _____ Pages _____

LESSON
4

The Powerful Presence of the Holy Spirit
Part Two

Lesson Objectives

Welcome in the strong name of Jesus Christ! After your reading, study, discussion, and application of the materials in this lesson, you will be able to:

*   Use the *RABBIS* acrostic to remember the work of the Holy Spirit in the lives of believers.

*   Explain the meaning and theological significance of the Spirit's role in gifting, indwelling, sealing, and sanctifying believers in Christ.

*   Identify key Scriptures which show that the work of the Holy Spirit is the means by which God gifts, indwells, seals and sanctifies believers in Christ.

Devotion

The Spirit Himself

Read Romans 8.26. Likewise the Spirit helps us in our weakness. For we do not know what to pray for as we ought, but the Spirit himself intercedes for us with groanings too deep for words.

[Read the devotion entitled "The Spirit Himself" from the course textbook *Names of the Holy Spirit*, pages 138-140.]

Nicene Creed and Prayer

After reciting and/or singing the Nicene Creed (located in the Appendix), pray the following prayer:

> *Breath into me, Holy Spirit, that my mind may turn to what is holy. Move me, Holy Spirit, that I may do what is holy. Strengthen me, Holy Spirit, that I may preserve what is holy. Protect me, Holy Spirit, that I may never lose what is holy. Amen.*

~ Saint Augustine, Bishop of Hippo and one of the
key theologians of the Church. He lived from 354 to 410 AD.
William Lane, S.J. **Praying with the Saints**. Dublin, Ireland: Veritas, 1989. p. 20.

4

Put away your notes, gather up your thoughts and reflections, and take the quiz for Lesson 3, *The Powerful Presence of the Holy Spirit (Part One)*.

Quiz

....

Review with a partner, write out and/or recite the text for last class session's assigned memory verse: Romans 8.22-25.

Scripture
Memorization
Review

....

Turn in your summary of the reading assignment for last week, that is, your brief response and explanation of the main points that the authors were seeking to make in the assigned reading (Reading Completion Sheet).

Assignments Due

....

CONTACT

Discussion: Spiritual Gifts

In their book *Soar With Your Strengths*, Donald Clifton and Paula Nelson tell a parable about a school that is held for the animals in a meadow. The teachers in the school believe that a well rounded animal can run, swim, climb trees, jump, and fly. When a rabbit enters the school the results are predictable, he does extremely well at running and jumping but horribly at swimming, tree climbing and flying. Naturally his teachers advise him to spend more time on the areas in which he is deficient. So the rabbit that used to spend his days running and jumping now spends his days working on swimming and flying and finds that he is constantly either humiliated or injured. The end result is that he hates school. In the end of the parable, however, he is inspired by a wise old owl to envision a world in which each person operates out of their strengths, gifts, and skills rather than trying to become what they were never intended to be.

In 1 Corinthians 12 the Apostle Paul makes a similar sort of analogy but instead of a parable about animals he uses the metaphor of the human body. Eyes see well but don't hear well. Ears hear well but have no sense of smell. The answer that Paul gives to this dilemma is not to try and make every body part do everything well but rather to encourage people to work together so that each person uses the gifts given to him or her by the Holy Spirit for the good of the whole body.

If this is true, it is very important that churches know and correctly use the spiritual gifts of their members. Speaking from your experience, how can we help the people in our congregations discover and use the gifts that the Spirit has given them?

Statement Completion Exercise: The Indwelling Holy Spirit

2 I am most aware that the Holy Spirit is living in me when . . . . .

After you have completed your answer, turn to a neighbor and take a few minutes to share with it with them and to listen to how they responded.

Singing about Sanctification

3 Songs and hymns are great ways to teach and learn scriptural truth. Later, we will be talking about the role of the Spirit in sanctifying us (setting us apart for God's use). This means that the Spirit is making us holy (that is like Jesus Christ) so that our words, actions, and attitudes reflect God's truth and character.

What are some songs or hymns that you sing in your church that speak about God's desire for us to be holy or his work in making us holy?

CONTENT

The Powerful Presence of the Holy Spirit (Part Two)

Segment 1: The Spirit Who Bestows Gifts and Indwells

Rev. Terry G. Cornett

4

Summary of Segment 1

Our objective for this segment, *The Spirit Who Bestows Gifts and Indwells*, is to enable you to:

- Understand the definition of spiritual gifts and be able to explain their purpose.

- Be able to identify, define, and categorize the spiritual gifts that are described in the New Testament.

- Identify and explain key theological principles associated with spiritual gifts.

- Describe the meaning and importance of the Spirit indwelling believers.

I.   The Spirit Who Bestows Gifts

A. Why are spiritual gifts necessary? Power for witness

1. Acts 1.8 - But you will receive power when the Holy Spirit has come upon you, and you will be my witnesses in Jerusalem and in all Judea and Samaria, and to the end of the earth.

2. The purpose of the Church is to be witnesses to what God has done, and is doing, in the world and the power for accomplishing this mission comes from the Holy Spirit. The Spirit gives gifts so that we can be a community that effectively spreads the good news that Jesus is Lord of all things. Even those gifts that are exercised completely inside of the Church and for the benefit of those who already know Christ exist for this same purpose. The Spirit gives gifts to strengthen the Church and its members but the reason the Church needs to be strengthened is so that it has the power to accomplish its mission in the world.

B. What are spiritual gifts?

1. *Charisma*: God's grace working in and through us

a. The word most commonly translated as "spiritual gift" is the Greek word *charisma*. This word comes from the Greek word for grace (*charis*) and literally means "gifts of grace." According to Romans 5.15-16, salvation itself is seen as the primary gift of grace—the gift from which all other gifts flow. But the word *charisma* or spiritual gift is used in a more specific way in a number of New Testament texts.

b. Rom. 12.4-8 - For as in one body we have many members, and the members do not all have the same function, [5] so we, though many, are one body in Christ, and individually members one of another. [6] Having gifts [*charismata*] that differ according to the grace given to us, let us use them: if prophecy, in proportion to our faith; [7] if service, in our serving; the one who teaches, in his teaching; [8] the one who exhorts, in his exhortation; the one who contributes, in generosity; the one who leads, with zeal; the one who does acts of mercy, with cheerfulness.

c. 1 Pet. 4.10 - As each has received a gift [*charisma*], use it to serve one another, as good stewards of God's varied grace.

d. 1 Cor. 12.4-6 - Now there are varieties of gifts [*charismata*], but the same Spirit; [5] and there are varieties of service, but the same Lord; [6] and there are varieties of activities, but it is the same God who empowers them all in everyone.

2. *Pneumatikos*: God's Spirit made visible in and through us

*Pneumatikos, the adj. formed from **pneuma**, conveys the sense of belonging to the realm of the spirit/Spirit, of the essence or nature of spirit/Spirit, embodying or manifesting the spirit/Spirit. . . . As a neut. noun, the spiritual, spiritual things. ~ "Spirit." The New International Dictionary of New Testament Theology, Vol. 3. Colin Brown, ed. Grand Rapids: Zondervan, 1986. pp. 706-707.*

a. 1 Cor. 12.1 - Now concerning spiritual gifts [*pneumatikoon*], brothers, I do not want you to be uninformed.

b. 1 Cor. 12.7 - To each is given the manifestation of the Spirit for the common good.

c. Even though in English, verse one speaks about spiritual gifts, the word for gift is not actually present in the original language. The word that is there would be more accurately translated "spirituals" (now concerning "spirituals" brothers, I do not want you to be uniformed). So what is he trying to say? If we read ahead to 1 Cor. 12.7, that verse helps us capture better what Paul means by

4

"spirituals": "To each is given the manifestation of the Spirit for the common good." Manifestation means that something is made clear or obvious. In other words, we can talk about spiritual gifts, not only as a specific kind of God given ability for ministry, but also as anything which makes the presence and the power of the Holy Spirit evident or visible. Therefore, an understanding of verse one in English might more understandably be written as, "Now concerning *manifestations of the Spirit*, brothers, I do not want you to be uninformed."

3. Toward a definition of spiritual gifts

   a. "Whatever thing, event, or individual serves as an instrument of the Spirit, or manifests the Spirit, or embodies the Spirit is a spiritual gift" (*Baker Encyclopedia of the Bible*).

   b. "A gift is a Spirit-given ability for Christian service" (Leslie B. Flynn, *19 Gifts of the Spirit*).

   c. "A spiritual gift is a gift of divine grace that is evidenced by some ability that benefits the body of Christ" (Thomas C. Oden, *Life in the Spirit*).

4. In all cases the purpose of spiritual gifts is to empower the Church to accomplish its mission in the world. Spiritual gifts, therefore, exist for the "common good" (1 Cor. 12.7) rather than for the individual.

C. "How many spiritual gifts are there?" and "What are these gifts?"

1. The key passages for studying spiritual gifts: each of these chapters include examples of some of the spiritual gifts and instructions for how they should be used in God's Church.

    a. Rom. 12

    b. 1 Cor. 12

    c. Eph. 4

    d. 1 Pet. 4

2. Inexhaustible gifts: there are an unlimited number of ways in which God's grace can work through us and in which God's Spirit can be revealed in us.

. . . .

Many people have tried to make out a list of the spiritual gifts discussed in the New Testament. This has often caused disagreement because each of the lists in the four major chapters on gifts is different and sometimes the same gift appears to be called by a different name. So if a person asks how many spiritual gifts there are, I would tell them that they are not asking the right question.

Since anything the Spirit does to make his power and presence visible in the lives of believers is a spiritual gift (manifestation), there are potentially an unlimited number of ways in which the Holy Spirit can gift people for ministry. However, it does seem clear that the Bible expects that, at the very least, the specific gifts that are mentioned in Scripture will be present in the Church (although not, perhaps, each gift in each congregation) and that these gifts will serve as a foundation for understanding how God empowers his Church to do his work.

It is not possible to name the number of the gifts which the church throughout the whole world has received from God, in the name of Jesus Christ . . .
~ Irenaeus quoted in *A Dictionary of Early Christian Beliefs.* David W. Bercot, ed. Peabody, MA: Henrickson, 1998. p. 299.

4

In light of this, the validity of any spiritual gift is established by its fidelity to the essential truths of Scripture (1 Thess 5.21; Jude 3), by its ability to build up the body of Christ (1 Cor. 14.12), and through its use being guided by true love for God and others (cf. 1 Cor. 13) in submission to legitimate church authority (Heb. 13.17).

~ Rev. Terry G. Cornett

. . . .

3. The gifts described in the New Testament

    a. For a description of these gifts see:

        (1) "Table of Spiritual Gifts Specifically Mentioned in the New Testament" (please refer to the Appendix of this workbook).

        (2) Craig S. Keener, *Gift and Giver*, pp. 113-136 (course text).

    b. Categorizing the gifts

    One thing that many people find helpful is to organize the spiritual gifts into categories that suggest what God is trying to doing through each gift. Theologians through the years have had many different ways of organizing but one I find especially helpful is to speak about word gifts, service gifts, power gifts, and leadership gifts.

        (1) Word Gifts

            (a) These are gifts that make God's *intentions* visible.

            (b) Among these gifts are discernment, evangelism, exhortation, knowledge, prophecy, teaching, and wisdom.

            (c) When these gifts are exercised in the Church, the people of God better understand God's plans, God's values, God's mission, and God's commands and are able to see more clearly how to obey them.

(2) Service gifts

    (a) These are gifts that make God's *heart* visible.

    (b) Among these gifts are celibacy (which gives a person the opportunity to put their entire life at the service of those in need), giving, mercy, and service (which is also called ministering, or helping).

    (c) When these gifts are exercised people directly experience the love of God being put into action to meet their needs. Through these gifts they understand how much God cares for them.

(3) Power gifts

    (a) These are gifts that make God's *supernatural presence* visible.

    (b) These gifts include faith, healing, miracles, tongues and interpretation.

    (c) When these gifts are exercised people see the Devil defeated, the destructive effects of sin overcome, and the purposes of God accomplished against great odds.

    (d) These gifts make it clear that God is real and active in the world today.

(4) Leadership gifts

    (a) These are gifts that make God's *purposes for a church* visible and bring them to completion.

    (b) Administration and Leadership. The office gifts: apostles, prophets, evangelists, pastors, teachers, elders, deacons (1 Cor. 12.28; Eph. 4; 1 Tim. 3.1-12).

    (c) When leadership gifts and offices are exercised, the Church is organized and equipped to fulfill its mission of proclaiming Jesus as Lord.

4

(d) Note - Only a few people will be called by God and authorized by the church to hold Christian leadership offices but all in the church are expected to use their gifts in active ministry to others.

D. Key theological principles concerning the gifts of the Spirit

1. *Every believer is given spiritual gifts which the Church needs to fulfill Christ's mission.*

   a. The direct teaching of Scripture

   (1) 1 Cor. 12.7

   (2) 1 Pet. 4.10

   b. The metaphor of the human body

   (1) 1 Cor. 12.14-30

   (2) Every part of the body is different and has its own unique function but each part is necessary for the whole body to work correctly. Likewise each person in Christ's body has different spiritual gifts and has their own unique function to play in the church but each person and their gifts are needed for the church to work correctly.

   c. Discovering your spiritual gifts: four key questions

   (1) What has God blessed?

   When you minister to people and they are helped, it is usually a sign that you are using your spiritual gift. Spiritual gifts bear fruit. Results are often a sign of giftedness.

(2) What brings you godly fulfillment?

Eph. 2.10 says, "For we are his workmanship, created in Christ Jesus for good works, which God prepared beforehand, that we should walk in them." When we do what we were created for it brings a sense of purpose and fulfillment. This doesn't mean that ministering in our spiritual gifts doesn't involve sacrifice, effort, and even frustration. It does mean that at the core of our being we know that we are fulfilling our God-given purpose and that we are taking our place in helping the Church fulfil the mission God has given it.

(3) What is the inner witness of the Holy Spirit?

The Spirit is the living, speaking voice of God. If the Spirit is the giver of gifts, he is also the one who guides us into understanding what our gifts are.

(4) What have others in your church (especially leaders) said about your gifts?

Spiritual gifts exist to strengthen and empower the Church so that it can accomplish its mission. In the long run, what you think about your gifts is far less important than what your congregation and its leadership thinks. They are the ones who know best of all whether the Holy Spirit is using you in a particular way to help them. It is a key job of pastors to help people determine what spiritual gifts each member has and to help them to develop and use those gifts in the most productive way. Ask your leaders what gifts they see in you and take their input seriously.

2. *The Holy Spirit alone decides which gifts each person will have.*

a. Believers have differing gifts.

(1) These gifts are distributed through the choice of the Holy Spirit, and they depend on other's gifts for completion and effectiveness.

(2) Rom. 12.6a

4

(3) 1 Cor. 12.11

(4) 1 Cor. 7.7

b. Gifts are not about status, 1 Cor. 12.20-22.

3. *Possessing a certain spiritual gift does not make a person more (or less) spiritual.*

a. 1 Corinthians 13: love, not gifting, is the measure of true spirituality.

The 1 Corinthians 13 passage suggests the true goal of the Spirit's indwelling is perfection in love. Exercise of the gifts that does not lead to this goal is not "of the Spirit" in Paul's mind. No act of power can, in and of itself, verify the work of the Spirit the way a single act of love can.

b. The Story of Balaam (Number 22-24)

The seer Balaam had the living presence of the Spirit of God come upon him in such a way that he prophesied under divine anointing (Num. 24.2-3) and even accurately foresaw the reign of God's Messiah in the distant future (Num. 24.17) but the Apostle Peter says that in God's estimation, Balaam was one who "loved the ways of wickedness" (2 Pet. 2.15). Spiritual gifts are rightly used by the mature person to accomplish God's purposes but they, in themselves, do nothing to make a person spiritually mature.

c. We are all "jars of clay," 2 Cor. 4.7.

The manifestation of God's power and presence is not about our spirituality but about his grace. No one deserves God's gracious gifts.

E. Review: the *RABBIS* acronym.

     1. He *Regenerates* us, making us brand new people.

     2. He *Adopts* us, causing us to belong to God's family and gain the full rights of family membership.

     3. He *Baptizes* us so that we are connected to other believers and filled with the power and holiness of God.

     4. He *Bestows* gifts that empower us to do God's work.

     5. He *Indwells* us with his living presence.

II. The Indwelling of the Holy Spirit

In the Old Testament God had a sanctuary for his people, in the New God has his people for a sanctuary.
~ Arthur Wallis

A. Definition: the indwelling of the Spirit is the means by which God is present with us at all times.

B. The Old Testament foundation

     1. The Tabernacle, Exod. 25.8

     2. The Pillar of Cloud and Fire, Exod. 13.21

C. The New Testament doctrine

The indwelling of the Holy Spirit is a distinctly New Testament doctrine. In the Old Testament there were visitations of the Spirit on individuals, as when God came upon a prophet or an artist to empower them for a specific ministry task. But in the New Testament, the Spirit is given as a permanent resident in the lives of those who accept Christ as Lord and Savior.

1. The teaching of Jesus, John 14.15-23 (cf. Matt. 18.18; 28.20)

2. The teaching of Paul

    a. The physical body of each Christian is indwelt by the Spirit, 1 Cor. 6.19.

    b. The Church corporately is the dwelling place of God's Spirit.

        (1) 1 Cor. 3.16

        (2) Eph. 2.18-22

3. The understanding of the Spirit as the paraclete.

    a. Paraclete

        (1) Literally, "one who is called alongside of another."

        (2) Metaphorically, a Comforter, Counselor, Helper, or Advocate

    b. Occurrences and implications:

        (1) To be with you forever, John 14.16

(2) "He will teach you all things and bring to your remembrance all that I have said to you," John 14.26.

(3) "He will bear witness about me," John 15.26.

(4) "It is to your advantage," John 16.7.

c. It only because of the Holy Spirit's ministry of indwelling that we can claim to know God, to hear his voice, and to experience his presence, Rom. 8.9.

D. Theological principles associated with the doctrine of indwelling

1. Intimacy

   a. Through the Spirit, God inhabits our bodies.

   b. The Spirit helps us in our weakness.

   c. The Spirit prays for and through us.

   d. The Spirit leads us into God's will.

   e. NOTE: The role of the Spirit in spiritual guidance is of fundamental importance. See "The Role of the Holy Spirit in Spiritual Guidance" in the appendix of this workbook for additional comments on this point.

2. Holiness

    a. The Church of Jesus Christ is the new temple of God with each member being a living stone (1 Pet. 2.5).

    b. Having been sprinkled with and purified by the blood of Christ (Hebrews 9 and 10), we are now able to experience the living presence of the HOLY Spirit.

    c. Like the Old Testament temple, the Church of God (corporately) and each of its members (individually) must be a place of holiness (Heb. 12).

Conclusion

» The Holy Spirit "Bestows Gifts" that *empower* God's people to build up the Church and accomplish his mission in the world. These gifts are the gracious power of God at work among us.

» The Holy Spirit "Indwells" believers so that the *living presence* of God the Father and God the Son are brought into their lives. Through the Spirit's indwelling, the Church becomes a temple of the Living God.

Please take as much time as you have available to answer these and other questions that the video brought out. You might want to start by reviewing the RABBIS acronym. Be clear and concise in your answers, and where possible, support with Scripture!

1. Why does the Holy Spirit give gifts to the Church?

2. How would you define the term "spiritual gift"?

3. How many spiritual gifts are there?

4. What is the relationship between spiritual gifts and natural talents?

Segue 1

Student Questions and Response

5. What is the relationship between spiritual gifts and spiritual maturity?

6. How does a person know what their spiritual gifts are?

7. Why would it be important for pastors to know the spiritual gifts of the people in their congregation?

8. How does the Tabernacle help us understand the indwelling of the Holy Spirit?

9. What does the Greek word *Paraclete* mean? How does it help us understand the indwelling work of the Holy Spirit?

10. Look briefly at Romans 8. What ministries of the indwelling Holy Spirit are described in this text?

The Powerful Presence of the Holy Spirit (Part Two)

Segment 2: The Spirit Who Seals and Sanctifies

Rev. Terry G. Cornett

Summary of Segment 2

In this segment we will look at the work of the Holy Spirit in sealing and sanctifying those who belong to Christ Jesus.

Our objective for this segment, *The Spirit Who Seals and Sanctifies*, is to enable you to see that:

- The Spirit of God is the one who transforms us into the image of Christ.

- Sanctification has a past, present, and future component.

- The Spirit of God is at war with evil.

- The fruit of the Spirit are key indicators of the life of Christ being reproduced in us.

- The Spirit's ministry of sealing provides us with assurance of our salvation.

4

I. The Spirit Who Sanctifies

A. Understanding the meaning of sanctification in Scripture

1. Definition

   a. Hebrew: *qādaš;* Greek: *hagiazō*

   In the Scriptures, the word "sanctify" literally means "to set apart for holy use." Anything that was reserved for God's use was sanctified.

   b. By implication "to sanctify" means: to make holy (free from anything that corrupts, defiles, or makes imperfect), pure, and blameless.

2. Scriptural examples:

   a. The Tabernacle and its furnishings (Exod. 40.9)

   b. The sacrificial animals (Lev. 22.21)

   c. The entire nation of Israel (Lev. 11.44)

   d. The New Testament Church (1 Cor. 1.2; 2 Cor. 6.16-18, 7.1)

4

3. The three stages of sanctification

The process of sanctification involves three elements: separating, purifying, and perfecting. Sanctification relates to the beginning [separating], the continuation [purifying], and the goal [perfecting] of the Christian life. Thus sanctification is past, present, and future.

~ J. Rodman Williams. **Renewal Theology.**

a. Theologians often use three separate words to define this one ongoing process of being set apart for God's use. Those words are justification, sanctification, and glorification. Therefore we can rightly say three things at once: we were sanctified [set apart for God's use], we are being sanctified [set apart for God's use], and we will be sanctified [set apart for God's use].

    (1) The beginning [separating] - *JUSTIFICATION*

        (a) Acts 26.18; Rom. 5.9; Gal. 2.16

        (b) NOTE: Justification means that we are declared to be righteous by God. It means that God no longer counts our sins against us but rather counts Christ's death for sin as paying our penalty in full. It wipes away our past rebellion and sets us apart from the world as people who no longer must face God's wrath against sin. Justification is the necessary first stage in the process of sanctification [being set apart for God]. See 1 Cor. 1.2; Heb. 10.14.

    (2) The continuation [purifying] - *SANCTIFICATION*

        (a) Rom. 6.19; 1 Thess. 5.23

        (b) NOTE: Having the Spirit teach us to live like Christ lived, so that our actions and attitudes are more and more holy, is what we most commonly call the process of sanctification in day-to-day life. As one theologian properly puts it, the most common use of the term sanctification in the New Testament is "the growth in holiness that should follow conversion."

4

(3) The goal [perfecting] - *GLORIFICATION*

    (a) Rom. 8.18; 1 John 3.2

    (b) NOTE: The end goal of our salvation is that we will have a new body, soul, and spirit which is freed from sin, sickness, and death, and we will live in a new world where God is King and righteousness reigns.

b. The goal of all sanctification is Christlikeness.

    (1) Rom. 8.29-30

    (2) 1 John 2.1-6

    (3) [Sanctification is] the work of God's free grace, whereby we are renewed in the whole man after the image of God, and are enabled more and more to die to sin and live unto righteousness (*The Westminister Catechism*).

B. The Spirit's work in sanctification

Although we are sinners, God substitutes Christ's holy life for our own. Christ's sinless life and death as a sacrifice for sin justified all who believe. Christ's holiness is substituted for their sinfulness. This is imputed holiness (justification). However, God does not intend to simply forgive our sins. He intends to transform us into holy people who actually become like his Son in our thoughts, words and actions. This is imparted holiness (sanctification). The Spirit is the one who actually gives us the desire to become holy and the power to live a holy life.

1. The Holy Spirit is at war with evil.

a. Cosmic: Everywhere in the universe that God's good rule and care is rebelled against, the Spirit is at work to restore things and make them right again.

> *Like the baptism in the Holy Spirit, the doctrine of sanctification has been a source of disagreement among Christians. Refer to the appendix for more information.*

b.   Personal: the Spirit is at war with the sinful nature that lives inside every person, Gal. 5.17.

*In Galatians 5.25, Paul gives advice about winning the war against sin. He says: "If we live by the Spirit, let us also walk by the Spirit." The term translated as "keeping in step," (or "walking" in some versions), is actually a military term [**stoicheo**] which describes soldiers keeping in step with a commanding officer as they march to battle.*

c.   The work of sanctification is portrayed in the language of military conflict.

(1)   Put on the "whole armor of God" and "and take the helmet of salvation, and the sword of the Spirit, which is the word of God, praying at all times in the Spirit, with all prayer and supplication," Eph. 6.

(2)   Col. 3.5

d.   We live "between the times": sanctification is "already" and "not yet."

(1)   Fact: we are sanctified and there is no need to sin, 1 John 2.1a.

(2)   Fact: Christians do sin and need forgiveness, 1 John 2.1b.

(3)   Fact: we are sanctified already, Heb. 10.14a.

(4)   Fact: we are still being sanctified, Heb. 10.14b.

(5)   Phil. 3.12-16

4

2.   The fruit of the Holy Spirit's presence in the believer is holy living.

a.   The Spirit is not only working to actively resist sin but also to actively produce Christlikeness.

b.   The fruit of the Spirit as a key measure of Christlikeness.

(1)   Gal. 5.22-24

(2)   The word translated "fruit" here is singular in the Greek. There are not different fruits of the Holy Spirit for us to pick and choose among. Wherever the Holy Spirit is doing his sanctifying work, all of these things will result.

C. Key theological principles concerning sanctification

1. Sanctification depends on Christ's work at Calvary but it is applied to each believer personally by the work of the Holy Spirit.

    a. What Christ did for us at the cross is the basis of what the Holy Spirit continues to do in us now. Faith in Christ is the source of both justification and sanctification.

       (1) Heb. 10.14

       (2) Rom. 3.24

    b. When we place our faith in Christ it is the Holy Spirit who comes to us to make us like him. The Spirit is the part of the Godhead that causes us to actually be transformed into righteous people.

       (1) 1 Cor. 6.9-11 (cf. 1 Thess. 4. 7-8)

       (2) Rom. 15.16

2. The Spirit's work always produces hatred of sin and increasing holiness of life. No Christian should come to accept sin as normal or inevitable.

    a. The Scriptures command holiness of life (Exod. 19.6; John 5.14; 1 Pet. 1.15-16). God would not command what was not possible or what he did not expect.

    b. The Scriptures promise holiness of life as a part of God's salvation (Deut. 30.6, Ezek. 36.25-27, Matt. 5.6; 1 Thess. 5.23-24). God would not promise something he does not intend to do.

4

3. Never despair of the Spirit's ability and willingness to make Christians holy.

    a. The mercy of Christ toward sinners (Matt. 18.21-22; 1 John 2.1) is always to be kept at the front of our minds. The Holy Spirit comes to us as the Spirit of Jesus (John 14.16-18; Phil. 1.19) who is the "friend of sinners."

    b. The Spirit is available to fill us over and over again so that we can constantly start afresh with new power in our battle against sin.

        (1) Eph. 5.18 - "Be filled with the Spirit"

        (2) This verb "be filled" is in the present, imperative tense (imperative simply means that it is a command). The present tense in Greek is used to show an action that happens continuously or is repeated over and over again.

4. The mature Christian will not rely on past victories but will stay constantly on guard against sin.

    a. There is no circumstance under which a Christian can legitimately claim to beyond the possibility of sinning.

        At the Council of Carthage (A.D. 418), the Church rejected the view that Christians do not sin. Those early Church fathers emphasized that the petitions found in the Lord's Prayer "Forgive us our trespasses" and "Lead us not into temptation" are requests that all Christians need to pray. They reasoned that if this is a prayer for all disciples, then no Christian can claim that they are so advanced in holiness that they are immune from temptation and sin.

Lest anyone should flatter himself that he is innocent–and should more deeply perish by exalting himself–he is instructed and taught that he sins daily. For he is told to pray daily for his sins.

~ Cyprian quoted in *A Dictionary of Early Christian Beliefs*. David W. Bercot, ed. Peabody, MA: Hendrickson, 1998. p. 618.

4

    b. The Scriptures teach that the person who is the most holy is also the most aware of their own sinfulness and most on guard against temptation.

        (1) 1 Cor. 10.12

        (2) Prov. 27.1-2 (cf. Job 9.20)

        (3) Isa. 6.5

        (4) Phil. 3.12-16

5. Suffering is a tool used by God in the process of sanctification.

    a. Ps. 119.67

    b. 1 Pet. 4.1

    c. Heb. 5.8

4

II. The Holy Spirit Who Seals Our Salvation

A. Seal: to set a mark upon a thing to show that it is authentic, accepted, or authoritative

1. The "seal" (*sphragis*) had various uses, all of which are instructive as applied to the Holy Spirit. It was affixed to a document to guarantee its genuineness. It was attached to goods in transit to indicate ownership and ensure protection. It also represented a designation of office in the state service (A. Skevington Wood, "Ephesians," *The Expositor's Bible Commentary*).

2. Definition: the presence and power of the Holy Spirit comes into our lives as God's seal which:

   a. Marks us as belonging to God (ownership)

   b. Places us under his authority (protection)

   c. Assures us that we will inherit what has been promised to us as joint-heirs with Christ (security).

B. Key texts

   1. Having believed, you were marked in him with a seal, the promised Holy Spirit, Eph. 1.13-14.

   2. Who has also put his seal on us and given us his Spirit in our hearts as a guarantee, 2 Cor. 1.21-22

   3. With whom you were sealed for the day of redemption, Eph. 4.30

C. Key theological implications concerning sealing

   1. Through sealing we receive assurance of our salvation.

      a. The power of God at work in us, Rom. 8.11

b. The presence of God speaking to us (the witness of the Spirit)

(1) The Spirit gives Scripture that forms the foundation of our confidence (objective witness), 1 John 5.13.

(2) The Spirit speaks to our spirit to assure us we belong to God (subjective witness).

(a) Rom. 8.16 (cf. 1 John 3.24; Acts 15.8)

(b) Gal. 4.6-7

(c) 1 John 3.24

2. The "witness of the Spirit"

a. The "witness of the Spirit" is the work of the Holy Spirit that gives the believer the clear awareness that he/she is reconciled to God.

(1) It is an inward and subjective knowledge that accompanies the objective knowledge from the Word.

(2) The testimony of the Spirit is an inward impression of the soul, whereby the Spirit of God directly witnesses to my spirit that I am a child of God, that Jesus Christ hath loved me, and given himself for me; and that all my sins are blotted out, and I, even I, am reconciled to God (John Wesley [Founder of Methodism]).

b. The Spirit also provides witness through our experiences of God after becoming a Christian. The experiences (in which God has acted in our lives with power) help us to remember and be assured of his continuing presence in our lives.

(1) Thus reassurance comes not only through the inner voice of the Spirit but also through his visible work in our lives. At the time the Roman centurion Cornelius accepted Christ he and his household experienced the gifts of tongues given by the Holy Spirit. As Peter looked back on that event he said, "And God,

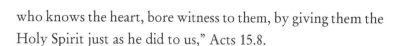

who knows the heart, bore witness to them, by giving them the Holy Spirit just as he did to us," Acts 15.8.

(2) Those who have served well gain an excellent standing and great assurance in their faith in Christ Jesus, 1 Tim. 3.13.

c. Experiencing doubts about whether we are saved does not mean that we do not possess the witness of the Spirit.

(1) 1 John 3.19-20

(2) A sensitive conscience and deep awareness of sin, guilt, and inadequacy is a sign of the Spirit's work. The person who has a "seared conscience (1 Tim. 4.1-2)" or "boasts of their own adequacy (Luke 18.11; John 9.41)" is the one who must be concerned about right relationship with God. The pastoral impulse is always to "comfort the afflicted" and "afflict the comfortable."

3. Sealing reminds us that our salvation is future as well as present.

a. And put his Spirit in our hearts as a deposit, guaranteeing what is to come, 2 Cor. 1.21-22

b. With whom you were sealed for the day of redemption, Eph. 4.30

c. Who are being saved, 1 Cor. 1.18 (cf. 2 Cor. 2.15).

d. Until the "day of the Lord" when Jesus returns to judge the world; conquer sin, death, and hell; give us new bodies, and recreate the heavens and the earth, we must live by faith and hope rather than sight and experience. The Holy Spirit allows us to taste the power of the "age to come" (Heb. 6.5) and his work in our life is a kind of first-fruit that assures us of the harvest to come.

Conclusion

» The Spirit is the one who "sanctifies and seals" those who place their faith in Jesus as Lord and Christ.

» In his work of sanctification, the Spirit applies Christ's victory over sin which was won at the cross to the life of each believer so that they are empowered to live holy lives.

» The Spirit is at work in the world to war against evil and to produce the fruit of righteousness.

» Although we live in a world where evil has not yet been eradicated by God's final day of judgment, the Holy Spirit has sealed those who have placed their faith in Christ Jesus so that they can know they belong to God, be assured of his presence, and recognize that they are under his protection during this evil age.

The following questions were designed to help you review the material in the second video segment. Again it may be helpful to start by reviewing the RABBIS acronym. Be clear and concise in your answers, and where possible, support with Scripture!

1. What does the word "sanctify" mean?

2. What similarities and differences are there between justification, sanctification, and glorification?

3. How would you counsel a person who claimed to be saved but did not demonstrate evidence of the fruit of the Spirit?

4. Are there any dangers in "striving for perfection"? If so, what? Are there any dangers in not "striving for perfection"? If so, what?

5. How is the ancient Roman wax seal (*sphragis*), a useful metaphor for understanding what the Holy Spirit does in the lives of Christians?

6. What is the "witness of the Spirit"?

Segue 2

Student Questions and Response

4

CONNECTION

Summary of Key Concepts

This lesson focuses upon the work of the Holy Spirit in empowering God people through gifts, through guidance (indwelling), through power over sin and the creation of Christlike character (sanctification), and through assuring the believer that they are included in God's ultimate victory over evil (sealing).

- Spiritual Gifts are given to empower the Church for mission.

- "Whatever thing, event, or individual serves as an instrument of the Spirit, or manifests the Spirit, or embodies the Spirit is a spiritual gift" (*Baker Encyclopedia of the Bible*).

- The key passages for studying spiritual gifts are Romans 12, 1 Corinthians 12, Ephesians 4, and 1 Peter 4.

- Every believer is given spiritual gifts which the Church needs to fulfill Christ's mission.

- The Holy Spirit alone decides which gifts each person will have: They are free gifts of "grace" and therefore those who receive them do not get special status or possess special spiritual maturity.

- Christian disagree about the definitions of some gifts, the relationship between spiritual gifts and natural talents, and whether all the spiritual gifts described in the New Testament are available today.

- The indwelling of the Holy Spirit in believers was prefigured by the Old Testament Tabernacle.

- The Spirit indwells his Church (corporately) and each believer (individually).

- The indwelling Spirit is the *paraclete*, the one called alongside as an advocate to guide, teach, encourage, and pray for us.

- Sanctification is the doctrine that describes being set apart for God's use. The goal of sanctification is complete Christlikeness.

- We are set apart for God's use through justification, sanctification, and glorification. Therefore, "sanctification" is past, present, and future.

- The Holy Spirit is always at war with evil.

- The fruit of the Spirit's sanctifying work in the life of the believer is holy living: conforming to Christ's teaching, example, and attitudes.

4

- The Spirit's work of sealing reminds us that our salvation is still yet to come (future) since it is not completely achieve until Christ returns and rules over a new heaven and a new earth.

- The witness of the Spirit describes the assurance given by the Spirit that we have been sealed and truly belong to Christ.

Student Application and Implications

Now is the time for you to discuss with your fellow students your questions about spiritual gifts, the indwelling of the Spirit, and the work of the Spirit in sealing and sanctifying those who belong to Christ. What particular questions do you have in light of the material you have just studied? Maybe some of the questions below might help you form your own, more specific and critical questions.

* Can true ministry occur that does not involve the use of spiritual gifts? Why or why not?

* What is the role of the pastor(s) in helping a person discover and use their spiritual gifts?

* Have disagreements arisen in your congregation about spiritual gifts? How were these disagreements resolved?

* How do we avoid giving the impression that certain spiritual gifts (for example, miracles or teaching) automatically mean that the person who has them is spiritually mature?

* What hope does a theology of spiritual gifts give to a person who is uneducated or impoverished?

* Should specific spiritual gifts be sought by a person? If so, on what basis? If not, why not?

* What are the implications of the Spirit's indwelling for individual believers? In what ways should our congregations recognize, celebrate, and respond to the presence of the Holy Spirit among us?

* What is the proper response to a member of a congregation who is habitually involved in a particular sin? Does the type of sin make any difference in formulating a response? Does the person's attitude and demeanor make any difference? Why or why not?

* How does a congregation show it is serious about issues of sin and holiness and yet avoid legalism and judgmentalism?

* What questions would you ask of, and what Scriptures would you refer to in counseling a Christian who was afraid that God no longer loved them or was with them?

CASE STUDIES

Got Gifts?

1 ▶ Randy has been a Christian for about a year. He has clearly grown in his in his love for God and others since he was converted. Randy does not read well but he has faithfully attended Bible studies and is eager to know the Scriptures. Although he has difficulty sharing the plan of salvation verbally, he has invited co-workers from the Wal-Mart he works at to attend church services with him and several of them have come. Last month the senior pastor preached a sermon series on spiritual gifts. Randy is eager to serve the church but feels like he just cannot figure out what his spiritual gifts are. He comes to you for advice and says "I'm not even sure that I have a spiritual gift. If I do, I definitely don't know how to find out what it is." What would you say to Randy?

Set Apart for God's Holy Use

2 ▶ Anita has had a difficult life. Her father sexually molested her from the time she was eight until she ran away from home at age sixteen. Once she was on the streets she turned to prostitution to support herself and to drugs to ease her pain and shame. Ten years ago she gave her life to Christ and started attending your church. After a glorious nine months of joy and freedom, old patterns began to reassert themselves. Since joining the church, Anita has been in drug rehab three times, has been arrested for prostitution once, and has stolen a number of items from the church and from church members. She will always be sorry for these actions later on and will try again to follow Christ. This usually lasts from between six months to a year before she is overcome by old sins again. If you were asked to counsel Anita and help her grow as a disciple of Christ, what would you do?

Signed, Sealed, Delivered, I'm Yours

Every pastor eventually is asked the following question. "How do I know that I have eternal life?" The person asking the question may be a brand new believer but could be someone who has been a church member for many years. Usually they are struggling with attacks by Satan that can include everything from doubts, inner accusations, to struggles with besetting sins. How would you answer that question?

The Holy Spirit is constantly at work to prepare God's people for works of service and witness. In this lesson we spoke about the way in which the Spirit qualifies them for service/witness by setting them apart and conforming them to the image of Christ (sanctification). We explored the way the Spirit empowers them for service/witness by manifesting his power through them (bestowing spiritual gifts). And finally, we spoke about the way in which the Spirit enables God's people to persevere in service/witness by sealing them and providing them with the assurance of God's presence that allows them to continue on in the face of doubts and uncertainty.

Restatement of the Lesson's Thesis

If you are interested in pursuing some of the ideas of *The Powerful Presence of the Holy Spirit (Part Two)*, you might want to give these books a try:

Resources and Bibliographies

Leslie B. Flynn. *19 Gifts of the Holy Spirit*. Wheaton, IL: Victor Books, 1994.

Harley H. Schmitt. *Many Gifts, One Lord*. Fairfax, VA: Xulon Press, 2002.

Alexander, Donald L, ed. *Christian Spirituality: Five Views of Sanctification*. Downers Grove, IL: InterVarsity Press, 1989.

You will be responsible to now apply the insights of your module in a practicum that you and your mentor agree to. The ramifications of doctrines concerning the person and work of the Holy Spirit are numerous and rich: think of all the ways that this teaching can influence your devotional life, your prayers, your response to your church, your attitude at work, and on and on and on. What is significant is that you seek to correlate this teaching with your life, work, and ministry. The ministry project is designed for this, and in the next days you will have the opportunity to share these insights in real-life, actual ministry environments. Pray that God will give you insight into his ways as you share your insights in your projects.

Ministry Connections

| Counseling and Prayer | Are there any issues, persons, situations, or opportunities that need to be prayed for as a result of your studies in this lesson? What particular issues or people has God laid upon your heart that require focused supplication and prayer for in this lesson? Take the time to ponder this, and receive the necessary support in counsel and prayer for what the Spirit has shown you. |

ASSIGNMENTS

| Scripture Memory | No assignment due. |

| Reading Assignment | No assignment due. |

| Other Assignments | Your ministry project and your exegetical project should now be outlined, determined, and accepted by your instructor. Make sure that you plan ahead, so you will not be late in turning in your assignments. |

| Final Exam Notice | The final will be a take home exam, and will include questions taken from the first three quizzes, new questions on material drawn from this lesson, and essay questions which will ask for your short answer responses to key integrating questions. Also, you should plan on reciting or writing out the verses memorized for the course on the exam. When you have completed your exam, please notify your mentor and make certain that they get your copy. |

Please note: Your module grade cannot be determined if you do not take the final exam and turn in all outstanding assignments to your mentor (reading completion sheets, ministry project, exegetical project, and final exam).

| The Last Word about this Module | In this module we have learned that the Holy Spirit is God himself, the third person of the one Trinitarian God. We have learned that he is not simply a force or power but a divine person who guides and instructs God's people. We have been reminded that he is the source of prophetic revelation and the means by which the inspired Scriptures came to us. We also saw that he is the one who convicts the world of sin and that it is impossible to recognize or come to the truth without being drawn to it by the work of the Holy Spirit. Finally, we used the *RABBIS* acrostic to remind |

4

ourselves of the major works of the Spirit in the life of the believer (*Regeneration, Adoption, Baptism, Bestowal of Gifts, Indwelling, Sealing,* and *Sanctifying*).

Perhaps the best course summary comes from St. Basil (329-379 AD):

> *Through the Holy Spirit comes our restoration to paradise, our ascension into the kingdom of heaven, our return to the adoption of sons, our liberty to call God our Father, our being made partakers of the grace of Christ, our being called children of light, our sharing in eternal glory and in a word, our being brought into a state of all "fullness of blessing, both in this world and in the world to come, of all the good gifts that are in store for us, by promise hereof, through faith, beholding the reflection of their grace as though they were already present, we await the full enjoyment.*

> ~ St. Basil. **On the Holy Spirit**. Chap. 15.

4

Appendices

APPENDIX 1
The Nicene Creed

We believe in one God,   *(Deut. 6.4-5; Mark 12.29; 1 Cor. 8.6)*
    the Father Almighty,   *(Gen. 17.1; Dan. 4.35; Matt. 6.9; Eph. 4.6; Rev. 1.8)*
    Maker of heaven and earth   *(Gen 1.1; Isa. 40.28; Rev. 10.6)*
    and of all things visible and invisible.   *(Ps. 148; Rom. 11.36; Rev. 4.11)*

We believe in one Lord Jesus Christ, the only Begotten Son of God,
    begotten of the Father before all ages,
    God from God, Light from Light, True God from True God,
    begotten not created,
    of the same essence as the Father,   *(John 1.1-2; 3.18; 8.58; 14.9-10; 20.28; Col. 1.15, 17; Heb. 1.3-6)*
    through whom all things were made.   *(John 1.3; Col. 1.16)*

Who for us men and for our salvation came down from heaven
    and was incarnate by the Holy Spirit and the virgin Mary
    and became human.   *(Matt. 1.20-23; John 1.14; 6.38; Luke 19.10)*
    Who for us too, was crucified under Pontius Pilate,
    suffered, and was buried.   *(Matt. 27.1-2; Mark 15.24-39, 43-47; Acts 13.29; Rom. 5.8; Heb. 2.10; 13.12)*
    The third day he rose again
    according to the Scriptures,   *(Mark 16.5-7; Luke 24.6-8; Acts 1.3; Rom. 6.9; 10.9; 2 Tim. 2.8)*
    ascended into heaven,
    and is seated at the right hand of the Father.   *(Mark 16.19; Eph. 1.19-20)*
    He will come again in glory
    to judge the living and the dead,
    and his Kingdom will have no end.
      (Isa. 9.7; Matt. 24.30; John 5.22; Acts 1.11; 17.31; Rom. 14.9; 2 Cor. 5.10; 2 Tim. 4.1)

We believe in the Holy Spirit, the Lord and life-giver,
    (Gen. 1.1-2; Job 33.4; Ps. 104.30; 139.7-8; Luke 4.18-19; John 3.5-6; Acts 1.1-2; 1 Cor. 2.11; Rev. 3.22)
    who proceeds from the Father and the Son,   *(John 14.16-18, 26; 15.26; 20.22)*
    who together with the Father and Son
    is worshiped and glorified,   *(Isa. 6.3; Matt. 28.19; 2 Cor. 13.14; Rev. 4.8)*
    who spoke by the prophets.   *(Num. 11.29; Mic. 3.8; Acts 2.17-18; 2 Pet. 1.21)*

We believe in one holy, catholic, and apostolic Church.
    (Matt. 16.18; Eph. 5.25-28; 1 Cor. 1.2; 10.17; 1 Tim. 3.15; Rev. 7.9)

We acknowledge one baptism for the forgiveness of sin,   *(Acts 22.16; 1 Pet. 3.21; Eph. 4.4-5)*
    And we look for the resurrection of the dead
    And the life of the age to come.   *(Isa. 11.6-10; Mic. 4.1-7; Luke 18.29-30; Rev. 21.1-5; 21.22-22.5)*

Amen.

APPENDIX 2

We Believe: Confession of the Nicene Creed (Common Meter*)

Rev. Dr. Don L. Davis, 2007. All Rights Reserved.

* This song is adapted from the Nicene Creed, and set to Common Meter (8.6.8.6.), meaning it can be sung to tunes of the same meter, such as: O, for a Thousand Tongues to Sing; Alas, and Did My Savior Bleed?; Amazing Grace; All Hail the Power of Jesus' Name; There Is a Fountain; Joy to the World

The Father God Almighty rules, Maker of earth and heav'n.
Yes, all things seen and those unseen, by him were made, and given!

We hold to one Lord Jesus Christ, God's one and only Son,
Begotten, not created, too, he and our Lord are one!

Begotten from the Father, same, in essence, God and Light;
Through him all things were made by God, in him were given life.

Who for us all, for salvation, came down from heav'n to earth,
Was incarnate by the Spirit's pow'r, and the Virgin Mary's birth.

Who for us too, was crucified, by Pontius Pilate's hand,
Suffered, was buried in the tomb, on third day rose again.

According to the Sacred text all this was meant to be.
Ascended to heav'n, to God's right hand, now seated high in glory.

He'll come again in glory to judge all those alive and dead.
His Kingdom rule shall never end, for he will reign as Head.

We worship God, the Holy Spirit, our Lord, Life-giver known,
With Fath'r and Son is glorified, Who by the prophets spoke.

And we believe in one true Church, God's people for all time,
Cath'lic in scope, and built upon the apostolic line.

Acknowledging one baptism, for forgiv'ness of our sin,
We look for Resurrection day–the dead shall live again.

We look for those unending days, life of the Age to come,
When Christ's great Reign shall come to earth, and God's will shall be done!

APPENDIX 3

The Story of God: Our Sacred Roots

Rev. Dr. Don L. Davis

The Alpha and the Omega	Christus Victor	Come, Holy Spirit	Your Word Is Truth	The Great Confession	His Life in Us	Living in the Way	Reborn to Serve
The LORD God is the source, sustainer, and end of all things in the heavens and earth. All things were formed and exist by his will and for his eternal glory, the triune God, Father, Son, and Holy Spirit, Rom. 11.36.							
THE TRIUNE GOD'S UNFOLDING DRAMA — God's Self-Revelation in Creation, Israel, and Christ				THE CHURCH'S PARTICIPATION IN GOD'S UNFOLDING DRAMA — Fidelity to the Apostolic Witness to Christ and His Kingdom			
The Objective Foundation: The Sovereign Love of God — *God's Narration of His Saving Work in Christ*				The Subjective Practice: Salvation by Grace through Faith — *The Redeemed's Joyous Response to God's Saving Work in Christ*			
The Author of the Story	*The Champion of the Story*	*The Interpreter of the Story*	*The Testimony of the Story*	*The People of the Story*	*Re-enactment of the Story*	*Embodiment of the Story*	*Continuation of the Story*
The Father as *Director*	Jesus as *Lead Actor*	The Spirit as *Narrator*	Scripture as *Script*	As Saints, *Confessors*	As Worshipers, *Ministers*	As Followers, *Sojourners*	As Servants, *Ambassadors*
Christian *Worldview*	Communal *Identity*	Spiritual *Experience*	Biblical *Authority*	Orthodox *Theology*	Priestly *Worship*	Congregational *Discipleship*	Kingdom *Witness*
Theistic and Trinitarian Vision	Christ-centered Foundation	Spirit-Indwelt and -Filled Community	Canonical and Apostolic Witness	Ancient Creedal Affirmation of Faith	Weekly Gathering in Christian Assembly	Corporate, Ongoing Spiritual Formation	Active Agents of the Reign of God
Sovereign *Willing*	Messianic *Representing*	Divine *Comforting*	Inspired *Testifying*	Truthful *Retelling*	Joyful *Excelling*	Faithful *Indwelling*	Hopeful *Compelling*
Creator — True Maker of the Cosmos	Recapitulation — Typos and Fulfillment of the Covenant	Life-Giver — Regeneration and Adoption	Divine Inspiration — God-breathed Word	The Confession of Faith — Union with Christ	Song and Celebration — Historical Recitation	Pastoral Oversight — Shepherding the Flock	Explicit Unity — Love for the Saints
Owner — Sovereign Disposer of Creation	Revealer — Incarnation of the Word	Teacher — Illuminator of the Truth	Sacred History — Historical Record	Baptism into Christ — Communion of Saints	Homilies and Teachings — Prophetic Proclamation	Shared Spirituality — Common Journey through the Spiritual Disciplines	Radical Hospitality — Evidence of God's Kingdom Reign
Ruler — Blessed Controller of All Things	Redeemer — Reconciler of All Things	Helper — Endowment and the Power	Biblical Theology — Divine Commentary	The Rule of Faith — Apostles' Creed and Nicene Creed	The Lord's Supper — Dramatic Re-enactment	Embodiment — Anamnesis and Prolepsis through the Church Year	Extravagant Generosity — Good Works
Covenant Keeper — Faithful Promisor	Restorer — Christ, the Victor over the powers of evil	Guide — Divine Presence and Shekinah	Spiritual Food — Sustenance for the Journey	The Vincentian Canon — Ubiquity, antiquity, universality	Eschatological Foreshadowing — The Already/Not Yet	Effective Discipling — Spiritual Formation in the Believing Assembly	Evangelical Witness — Making Disciples of All People Groups

APPENDIX 4

The Theology of Christus Victor

A Christ-Centered Biblical Motif for Integrating and Renewing the Urban Church

Rev. Dr. Don L. Davis

	The Promised Messiah	The Word Made Flesh	The Son of Man	The Suffering Servant	The Lamb of God	The Victorious Conqueror	The Reigning Lord in Heaven	The Bridegroom and Coming King
Biblical Framework	Israel's hope of Yahweh's anointed who would redeem his people	In the person of Jesus of Nazareth, the Lord has come to the world	As the promised king and divine Son of Man, Jesus reveals the Father's glory and salvation to the world	As Inaugurator of the Kingdom of God, Jesus demonstrates God's reign present through his words, wonders, and works	As both High Priest and Paschal Lamb, Jesus offers himself to God on our behalf as a sacrifice for sin	In his resurrection from the dead and ascension to God's right hand, Jesus is proclaimed as Victor over the power of sin and death	Now reigning at God's right hand till his enemies are made his footstool, Jesus pours out his benefits on his body	Soon the risen and ascended Lord will return to gather his Bride, the Church, and consummate his work
Scripture References	Isa. 9.6-7 Jer. 23.5-6 Isa. 11.1-10	John 1.14-18 Matt. 1.20-23 Phil. 2.6-8	Matt. 2.1-11 Num. 24.17 Luke 1.78-79	Mark 1.14-15 Matt. 12.25-30 Luke 17.20-21	2 Cor. 5.18-21 Isa. 52-53 John 1.29	Eph. 1.16-23 Phil. 2.5-11 Col. 1.15-20	1 Cor. 15.25 Eph. 4.15-16 Acts. 2.32-36	Rom. 14.7-9 Rev. 5.9-13 1 Thess. 4.13-18
Jesus' History	The pre-incarnate, only begotten Son of God in glory	His conception by the Spirit, and birth to Mary	His manifestation to the Magi and to the world	His teaching, exorcisms, miracles, and mighty works among the people	His suffering, crucifixion, death, and burial	His resurrection, with appearances to his witnesses, and his ascension to the Father	The sending of the Holy Spirit and his gifts, and Christ's session in heaven at the Father's right hand	His soon return from heaven to earth as Lord and Christ: the Second Coming
Description	The biblical promise for the seed of Abraham, the prophet like Moses, the son of David	In the Incarnation, God has come to us; Jesus reveals to humankind the Father's glory in fullness	In Jesus, God has shown his salvation to the entire world, including the Gentiles	In Jesus, the promised Kingdom of God has come visibly to earth, demonstrating his binding of Satan and rescinding the Curse	As God's perfect Lamb, Jesus offers himself up to God as a sin offering on behalf of the entire world	In his resurrection and ascension, Jesus destroyed death, disarmed Satan, and rescinded the Curse	Jesus is installed at the Father's right hand as Head of the Church, Firstborn from the dead, and supreme Lord in heaven	As we labor in his harvest field in the world, so we await Christ's return, the fulfillment of his promise
Church Year	Advent	Christmas	Season after Epiphany Baptism and Transfiguration	Lent	Holy Week Passion	Eastertide Easter, Ascension Day, Pentecost	Season after Pentecost Trinity Sunday	Season after Pentecost All Saints Day, Reign of Christ the King
	The Coming of Christ	*The Birth of Christ*	*The Manifestation of Christ*	*The Ministry of Christ*	*The Suffering and Death of Christ*	*The Resurrection and Ascension of Christ*	*The Heavenly Session of Christ*	*The Reign of Christ*
Spiritual Formation	As we await his Coming, let us proclaim and affirm the hope of Christ	O Word made flesh, let us every heart prepare him room to dwell	Divine Son of Man, show the nations your salvation and glory	In the person of Christ, the power of the reign of God has come to earth and to the Church	May those who share the Lord's death be resurrected with him	Let us participate by faith in the victory of Christ over the power of sin, Satan, and death	Come, indwell us, Holy Spirit, and empower us to advance Christ's Kingdom in the world	We live and work in expectation of his soon return, seeking to please him in all things

APPENDIX 5

Christus Victor

An Integrated Vision for the Christian Life

Rev. Dr. Don L. Davis

For the Church

- The Church is the primary extension of Jesus in the world
- Ransomed treasure of the victorious, risen Christ
- *Laos:* The people of God
- God's new creation: presence of the future
- Locus and agent of the Already/Not Yet Kingdom

For Theology and Doctrine

- The authoritative Word of Christ's victory: the Apostolic Tradition: the Holy Scriptures
- Theology as commentary on the grand narrative of God
- *Christus Victor* as core theological framework for meaning in the world
- The Nicene Creed: the Story of God's triumphant grace

For Spirituality

- The Holy Spirit's presence and power in the midst of God's people
- Sharing in the disciplines of the Spirit
- Gatherings, lectionary, liturgy, and our observances in the Church Year
- Living the life of the risen Christ in the rhythm of our ordinary lives

For Gifts

- God's gracious endowments and benefits from *Christus Victor*
- Pastoral offices to the Church
- The Holy Spirit's sovereign dispensing of the gifts
- Stewardship: divine, diverse gifts for the common good

Christus Victor

Destroyer of Evil and Death
Restorer of Creation
Victor o'er Hades and Sin
Crusher of Satan

For Worship

- People of the Resurrection: unending celebration of the people of God
- Remembering, participating in the Christ event in our worship
- Listen and respond to the Word
- Transformed at the Table, the Lord's Supper
- The presence of the Father through the Son in the Spirit

For Evangelism and Mission

- Evangelism as unashamed declaration and demonstration of *Christus Victor* to the world
- The Gospel as Good News of kingdom pledge
- We proclaim God's Kingdom come in the person of Jesus of Nazareth
- The Great Commission: go to all people groups making disciples of Christ and his Kingdom
- Proclaiming Christ as Lord and Messiah

For Justice and Compassion

- The gracious and generous expressions of Jesus through the Church
- The Church displays the very life of the Kingdom
- The Church demonstrates the very life of the Kingdom of heaven right here and now
- Having freely received, we freely give (no sense of merit or pride)
- Justice as tangible evidence of the Kingdom come

APPENDIX 6

Old Testament Witness to Christ and His Kingdom

Rev. Dr. Don L. Davis

Christ Is Seen in the OT's:	Covenant Promise and Fulfillment	Moral Law	Christophanies	Typology	Tabernacle, Festival, and Levitical Priesthood	Messianic Prophecy	Salvation Promises
Passage	Gen. 12.1-3	Matt. 5.17-18	John 1.18	1 Cor. 15.45	Heb. 8.1-6	Mic. 5.2	Isa. 9.6-7
Example	The Promised Seed of the Abrahamic covenant	The Law given on Mount Sinai	Commander of the Lord's army	Jonah and the great fish	Melchizedek, as both High Priest and King	The Lord's Suffering Servant	Righteous Branch of David
Christ As	Seed of the woman	The Prophet of God	God's present Revelation	Antitype of God's drama	Our eternal High Priest	The coming Son of Man	Israel's Redeemer and King
Where Illustrated	Galatians	Matthew	John	Matthew	Hebrews	Luke and Acts	John and Revelation
Exegetical Goal	To see Christ as heart of God's sacred drama	To see Christ as fulfillment of the Law	To see Christ as God's revealer	To see Christ as antitype of divine typos	To see Christ in the Temple *cultus*	To see Christ as true Messiah	To see Christ as coming King
How Seen in the NT	As fulfillment of God's sacred oath	As *telos* of the Law	As full, final, and superior revelation	As substance behind the historical shadows	As reality behind the rules and roles	As the Kingdom made present	As the One who will rule on David's throne
Our Response in Worship	God's veracity and faithfulness	God's perfect righteousness	God's presence among us	God's inspired Scripture	God's ontology: his realm as primary and determinative	God's anointed servant and mediator	God's resolve to restore his kingdom authority
How God Is Vindicated	God does not lie: he's true to his word	Jesus fulfills all righteousness	God's fulness is revealed to us in Jesus of Nazareth	The Spirit spoke by the prophets	The Lord has provided a mediator for humankind	Every jot and tittle written of him will occur	Evil will be put down, creation restored, under his reign

APPENDIX 7

Summary Outline of the Scriptures

Rev. Dr. Don L. Davis

1. GENESIS - Beginnings
   a. Adam
   b. Noah
   c. Abraham
   d. Isaac
   e. Jacob
   f. Joseph

2. EXODUS - Redemption, (out of)
   a. Slavery
   b. Deliverance
   c. Law
   d. Tabernacle

3. LEVITICUS - Worship and Fellowship
   a. Offerings, sacrifices
   b. Priests
   c. Feasts, festivals

4. NUMBERS - Service and Walk
   a. Organized
   b. Wanderings

5. DEUTERONOMY - Obedience
   a. Moses reviews history and law
   b. Civil and social laws
   c. Palestinian Covenant
   d. Moses' blessing and death

6. JOSHUA - Redemption (into)
   a. Conquer the land
   b. Divide up the land
   c. Joshua's farewell

7. JUDGES - God's Deliverance
   a. Disobedience and judgment
   b. Israel's twelve judges
   c. Lawless conditions

8. RUTH - Love
   a. Ruth chooses
   b. Ruth works
   c. Ruth waits
   d. Ruth rewarded

9. 1 SAMUEL - Kings, Priestly Perspective
   a. Eli
   b. Samuel
   c. Saul
   d. David

10. 2 SAMUEL - David
    a. King of Judah
       (9 years - Hebron)
    b. King of all Israel
       (33 years - Jerusalem)

11. 1 KINGS - Solomon's Glory, Kingdom's Decline
    a. Solomon's glory
    b. Kingdom's decline
    c. Elijah the prophet

12. 2 KINGS- Divided Kingdom
    a. Elisha
    b. Israel (N. Kingdom falls)
    c. Judah (S. Kingdom falls)

13. 1 CHRONICLES - David's Temple Arrangements
    a. Genealogies
    b. End of Saul's reign
    c. Reign of David
    d. Temple preparations

14. 2 CHRONICLES - Temple and Worship Abandoned
    a. Solomon
    b. Kings of Judah

15. EZRA - The Minority (Remnant)
    a. First return from exile - Zerubbabel
    b. Second return from exile - Ezra (priest)

16. NEHEMIAH - Rebuilding by Faith
    a. Rebuild walls
    b. Revival
    c. Religious reform

17. ESTHER - Female Savior
    a. Esther
    b. Haman
    c. Mordecai
    d. Deliverance: Feast of Purim

18. JOB - Why the Righteous Suffer
    a. Godly Job
    b. Satan's attack
    c. Four philosophical friends
    d. God lives

19. PSALMS - Prayer and Praise
    a. Prayers of David
    b. Godly suffer; deliverance
    c. God deals with Israel
    d. Suffering of God's people - end with the Lord's reign
    e. The Word of God (Messiah's suffering and glorious return)

20. PROVERBS - Wisdom
    a. Wisdom versus folly
    b. Solomon
    c. Solomon - Hezekiah
    d. Agur
    e. Lemuel

21. ECCLESIASTES - Vanity
    a. Experimentation
    b. Observation
    c. Consideration

22. SONG OF SOLOMON - Love Story

23. ISAIAH - The Justice (Judgment) and Grace (Comfort) of God
    a. Prophecies of punishment
    b. History
    c. Prophecies of blessing

24. JEREMIAH - Judah's Sin Leads to Babylonian Captivity
    a. Jeremiah's call; empowered
    b. Judah condemned; predicted Babylonian captivity
    c. Restoration promised
    d. Prophesied judgment inflicted
    e. Prophesies against Gentiles
    f. Summary of Judah's captivity

25. LAMENTATIONS - Lament over Jerusalem
    a. Affliction of Jerusalem
    b. Destroyed because of sin
    c. The prophet's suffering
    d. Present desolation versus past splendor
    e. Appeal to God for mercy

26. EZEKIEL - Israel's Captivity and Restoration
    a. Judgment on Judah and Jerusalem
    b. Judgment on Gentile nations
    c. Israel restored; Jerusalem's future glory

27. DANIEL - The Time of the Gentiles
    a. History; Nebuchadnezzar, Belshazzar, Daniel
    b. Prophecy

28. HOSEA - Unfaithfulness
    a. Unfaithfulness
    b. Punishment
    c. Restoration

29. JOEL - The Day of the Lord
    a. Locust plague
    b. Events of the future day of the Lord
    c. Order of the future day of the Lord

30. AMOS - God Judges Sin
    a. Neighbors judged
    b. Israel judged
    c. Visions of future judgment
    d. Israel's past judgment blessings

31. OBADIAH - Edom's Destruction
    a. Destruction prophesied
    b. Reasons for destruction
    c. Israel's future blessing

32. JONAH - Gentile Salvation
    a. Jonah disobeys
    b. Other suffer
    c. Jonah punished
    d. Jonah obeys; thousands saved
    e. Jonah displeased, no love for souls

33. MICAH - Israel's Sins, Judgment, and Restoration
    a. Sin and judgment
    b. Grace and future restoration
    c. Appeal and petition

34. NAHUM - Nineveh Condemned
    a. God hates sin
    b. Nineveh's doom prophesied
    c. Reasons for doom

35. HABAKKUK - The Just Shall Live by Faith
    a. Complaint of Judah's unjudged sin
    b. Chaldeans will punish
    c. Complaint of Chaldeans' wickedness
    d. Punishment promised
    e. Prayer for revival; faith in God

36. ZEPHANIAH - Babylonian Invasion Prefigures the Day of the Lord
    a. Judgment on Judah foreshadows the Great Day of the Lord
    b. Judgment on Jerusalem and neighbors foreshadows final judgment of all nations
    c. Israel restored after judgments

37. HAGGAI - Rebuild the Temple
    a. Negligence
    b. Courage
    c. Separation
    d. Judgment

38. ZECHARIAH - Two Comings of Christ
    a. Zechariah's vision
    b. Bethel's question; Jehovah's answer
    c. Nation's downfall and salvation

39. MALACHI - Neglect
    a. The priest's sins
    b. The people's sins
    c. The faithful few

Summary Outline of the Scriptures (continued)

1. MATTHEW - Jesus the King
   a. The Person of the King
   b. The Preparation of the King
   c. The Propaganda of the King
   d. The Program of the King
   e. The Passion of the King
   f. The Power of the King

2. MARK - Jesus the Servant
   a. John introduces the Servant
   b. God the Father identifies the Servant
   c. The temptation initiates the Servant
   d. Work and word of the Servant
   e. Death, burial, resurrection

3. LUKE - Jesus Christ the Perfect Man
   a. Birth and family of the Perfect Man
   b. Testing of the Perfect Man; hometown
   c. Ministry of the Perfect Man
   d. Betrayal, trial, and death of the Perfect Man
   e. Resurrection of the Perfect Man

4. JOHN - Jesus Christ is God
   a. Prologue - the Incarnation
   b. Introduction
   c. Witness of Jesus to his Apostles
   d. Passion - witness to the world
   e. Epilogue

5. ACTS - The Holy Spirit Working in the Church
   a. The Lord Jesus at work by the Holy Spirit through the Apostles at Jerusalem
   b. In Judea and Samaria
   c. To the uttermost parts of the Earth

6. ROMANS - The Righteousness of God
   a. Salutation
   b. Sin and salvation
   c. Sanctification
   d. Struggle
   e. Spirit-filled living
   f. Security of salvation
   g. Segregation
   h. Sacrifice and service
   i. Separation and salutation

7. 1 CORINTHIANS - The Lordship of Christ
   a. Salutation and thanksgiving
   b. Conditions in the Corinthian body
   c. Concerning the Gospel
   d. Concerning collections

8. 2 CORINTHIANS - The Ministry in the Church
   a. The comfort of God
   b. Collection for the poor
   c. Calling of the Apostle Paul

9. GALATIANS - Justification by Faith
   a. Introduction
   b. Personal - Authority of the Apostle and glory of the Gospel
   c. Doctrinal - Justification by faith
   d. Practical - Sanctification by the Holy Spirit
   e. Autographed conclusion and exhortation

10. EPHESIANS - The Church of Jesus Christ
    a. Doctrinal - the heavenly calling of the Church
       A Body
       A Temple
       A Mystery
    b. Practical - The earthly conduct of the Church
       A New Man
       A Bride
       An Army

11. PHILIPPIANS - Joy in the Christian Life
    a. Philosophy for Christian living
    b. Pattern for Christian living
    c. Prize for Christian living
    d. Power for Christian living

12. COLOSSIANS - Christ the Fullness of God
    a. Doctrinal - In Christ believers are made full
    b. Practical - Christ's life poured out in believers, and through them

13. 1 THESSALONIANS - The Second Coming of Christ:
    a. Is an inspiring hope
    b. Is a working hope
    c. Is a purifying hope
    d. Is a comforting hope
    e. Is a rousing, stimulating hope

14. 2 THESSALONIANS - The Second Coming of Christ
    a. Persecution of believers now; judgment of unbelievers hereafter (at coming of Christ)
    b. Program of the world in connection with the coming of Christ
    c. Practical issues associated with the coming of Christ

15. 1 TIMOTHY - Government and Order in the Local Church
    a. The faith of the Church
    b. Public prayer and women's place in the Church
    c. Officers in the Church
    d. Apostasy in the Church
    e. Duties of the officer of the Church

16. 2 TIMOTHY - Loyalty in the Days of Apostasy
    a. Afflictions of the Gospel
    b. Active in service
    c. Apostasy coming; authority of the Scriptures
    d. Allegiance to the Lord

17. TITUS - The Ideal New Testament Church
    a. The Church is an organization
    b. The Church is to teach and preach the Word of God
    c. The Church is to perform good works

18. PHILEMON - Reveal Christ's Love and Teach Brotherly Love
    a. Genial greeting to Philemon and family
    b. Good reputation of Philemon
    c. Gracious plea for Onesimus
    d. Guiltless illustration of Imputation
    e. General and personal requests

19. HEBREWS - The Superiority of Christ
    a. Doctrinal - Christ is better than the Old Testament economy
    b. Practical - Christ brings better benefits and duties

20. JAMES - Ethics of Christianity
    a. Faith tested
    b. Difficulty of controlling the tongue
    c. Warning against worldliness
    d. Admonitions in view of the Lord's coming

21. 1 PETER - Christian Hope in the Time of Persecution and Trial
    a. Suffering and security of believers
    b. Suffering and the Scriptures
    c. Suffering and the sufferings of Christ
    d. Suffering and the Second Coming of Christ

22. 2 PETER - Warning Against False Teachers
    a. Addition of Christian graces gives assurance
    b. Authority of the Scriptures
    c. Apostasy brought in by false testimony
    d. Attitude toward Return of Christ: test for apostasy
    e. Agenda of God in the world
    f. Admonition to believers

23. 1 JOHN - The Family of God
    a. God is Light
    b. God is Love
    c. God is Life

24. 2 JOHN - Warning against Receiving Deceivers
    a. Walk in truth
    b. Love one another
    c. Receive not deceivers
    d. Find joy in fellowship

25. 3 JOHN - Admonition to Receive True Believers
    a. Gaius, brother in the Church
    b. Diotrephes
    c. Demetrius

26. JUDE - Contending for the Faith
    a. Occasion of the epistle
    b. Occurrences of apostasy
    c. Occupation of believers in the days of apostasy

27. REVELATION - The Unveiling of Christ Glorified
    a. The person of Christ in glory
    b. The possession of Jesus Christ - the Church in the World
    c. The program of Jesus Christ - the scene in Heaven
    d. The seven seals
    e. The seven trumpets
    f. Important persons in the last days
    g. The seven vials
    h. The fall of Babylon
    i. The eternal state

APPENDIX 8

From Before to Beyond Time:
The Plan of God and Human History
*Adapted from: Suzanne de Dietrich. **God's Unfolding Purpose**. Philadelphia: Westminster Press, 1976.*

I. Before Time (Eternity Past) 1 Cor. 2.7
   A. The Eternal Triune God
   B. God's Eternal Purpose
   C. The Mystery of Iniquity
   D. The Principalities and Powers

II. Beginning of Time (Creation and Fall) Gen. 1.1
   A. Creative Word
   B. Humanity
   C. Fall
   D. Reign of Death and First Signs of Grace

III. Unfolding of Time (God's Plan Revealed Through Israel) Gal. 3.8
   A. Promise (Patriarchs)
   B. Exodus and Covenant at Sinai
   C. Promised Land
   D. The City, the Temple, and the Throne (Prophet, Priest, and King)
   E. Exile
   F. Remnant

IV. Fullness of Time (Incarnation of the Messiah) Gal. 4.4-5
   A. The King Comes to His Kingdom
   B. The Present Reality of His Reign
   C. The Secret of the Kingdom: the Already and the Not Yet
   D. The Crucified King
   E. The Risen Lord

V. The Last Times (The Descent of the Holy Spirit) Acts 2.16-18
   A. Between the Times: the Church as Foretaste of the Kingdom
   B. The Church as Agent of the Kingdom
   C. The Conflict Between the Kingdoms of Darkness and Light

VI. The Fulfillment of Time (The Second Coming) Matt. 13.40-43
   A. The Return of Christ
   B. Judgment
   C. The Consummation of His Kingdom

VII. Beyond Time (Eternity Future) 1 Cor. 15.24-28
   A. Kingdom Handed Over to God the Father
   B. God as All in All

From Before to Beyond Time
Scriptures for Major Outline Points

I. Before Time (Eternity Past)

1 Cor. 2.7 (ESV) - But we impart a secret and hidden wisdom of God, *which God decreed before the ages* for our glory (cf. Titus 1.2).

II. Beginning of Time (Creation and Fall)

Gen. 1.1 (ESV) - *In the beginning*, God created the heavens and the earth.

III. Unfolding of Time (God's Plan Revealed Through Israel)

Gal. 3.8 (ESV) - And the Scripture, foreseeing that God would justify the Gentiles by faith, *preached the Gospel beforehand to Abraham*, saying, "In you shall all the nations be blessed" (cf. Rom. 9.4-5).

IV. Fullness of Time (The Incarnation of the Messiah)

Gal. 4.4-5 (ESV) - *But when the fullness of time had come*, God sent forth his Son, born of woman, born under the law, to redeem those who were under the law, so that we might receive adoption as sons.

V. The Last Times (The Descent of the Holy Spirit)

Acts 2.16-18 (ESV) - But this is what was uttered through the prophet Joel: "'*And in the last days it shall be*,' God declares, 'that I will pour out my Spirit on all flesh, and your sons and your daughters shall prophesy, and your young men shall see visions, and your old men shall dream dreams; even on my male servants and female servants in those days I will pour out my Spirit, and they shall prophesy.'"

VI. The Fulfillment of Time (The Second Coming)

Matt. 13.40-43 (ESV) - Just as the weeds are gathered and burned with fire, *so will it be at the close of the age*. The Son of Man will send his angels, and they will gather out of his kingdom all causes of sin and all lawbreakers, and throw them into the fiery furnace. In that place there will be weeping and gnashing of teeth. Then the righteous will shine like the sun in the Kingdom of their Father. He who has ears, let him hear.

VII. Beyond Time (Eternity Future)

1 Cor. 15.24-28 (ESV) - Then comes the end, when he delivers the Kingdom to God the Father after destroying every rule and every authority and power. For he must reign until he has put all his enemies under his feet. The last enemy to be destroyed is death. For "God has put all things in subjection under his feet." But when it says, "all things are put in subjection," it is plain that he is excepted who put all things in subjection under him. When all things are subjected to him, then the Son himself will also be subjected to him who put all things in subjection under him, that God may be all in all.

APPENDIX 9

"There Is a River"

Identifying the Streams of a Revitalized Authentic Christian Community in the City[1]

Rev. Dr. Don L. Davis   •   Psalm 46.4 (ESV) - There is a river whose streams make glad the city of God, the holy habitation of the Most High.

Tributaries of Authentic Historic Biblical Faith			
Recognized Biblical Identity	*Revived Urban Spirituality*	*Reaffirmed Historical Connectivity*	*Refocused Kingdom Authority*
The Church Is **One**	The Church Is **Holy**	The Church Is **Catholic**	The Church Is **Apostolic**
A Call to Biblical Fidelity *Recognizing the Scriptures as the anchor and foundation of the Christian faith and practice*	A Call to the Freedom, Power, and Fullness of the Holy Spirit *Walking in the holiness, power, gifting, and liberty of the Holy Spirit in the body of Christ*	A Call to Historic Roots and Continuity *Confessing the common historical identity and continuity of authentic Christian faith*	A Call to the Apostolic Faith *Affirming the apostolic tradition as the authoritative ground of the Christian hope*
A Call to Messianic Kingdom Identity *Rediscovering the story of the promised Messiah and his Kingdom in Jesus of Nazareth*	A Call to Live as Sojourners and Aliens as the People of God *Defining authentic Christian discipleship as faithful membership among God's people*	A Call to Affirm and Express the Global Communion of Saints *Expressing cooperation and collaboration with all other believers, both local and global*	A Call to Representative Authority *Submitting joyfully to God's gifted servants in the Church as undershepherds of true faith*
A Call to Creedal Affinity *Embracing the Nicene Creed as the shared rule of faith of historic orthodoxy*	A Call to Liturgical, Sacramental, and Catechetical Vitality *Experiencing God's presence in the context of the Word, sacrament, and instruction*	A Call to Radical Hospitality and Good Works *Expressing kingdom love to all, and especially to those of the household of faith*	A Call to Prophetic and Holistic Witness *Proclaiming Christ and his Kingdom in word and deed to our neighbors and all peoples*

[1] *This schema is an adaptation and is based on the insights of the **Chicago Call** statement of May 1977, where various leading evangelical scholars and practitioners met to discuss the relationship of modern evangelicalism to the historic Christian faith.*

APPENDIX 10

A Schematic for a Theology of the Kingdom and the Church

The Urban Ministry Institute

The Reign of the One, True, Sovereign, and Triune God, the LORD God, Yahweh, God the Father, Son, and Holy Spirit

	The Father	The Son	The Spirit
	Love - 1 John 4.8 Maker of heaven and earth and of all things visible and invisible	Faith - Heb. 12.2 Prophet, Priest, and King	Hope - Rom. 15.13 Lord of the Church
	Creation All that exists through the creative action of God.	**Kingdom** The Reign of God expressed in the rule of his Son Jesus the Messiah.	**Church** The one, holy, apostolic community which functions as a witness to (Acts 28.31) and a foretaste of (Col. 1.12; James 1.18; 1 Pet. 2.9; Rev. 1.6) the Kingdom of God.
Rom. 8.18-21 →	The eternal God, sovereign in power, infinite in wisdom, perfect in holiness, and steadfast in love, is the source and goal of all things.	**Freedom** (Slavery) Jesus answered them, "Truly, truly, I say to you, everyone who commits sin is a slave to sin. The slave does not remain in the house forever; the son remains forever. So if the Son sets you free, you will be free indeed." - John 8.34-36(ESV)	*The Church is an Apostolic Community Where the Word is Rightly Preached, Therefore it is a Community of:* **Calling** - For freedom Christ has set us free; stand firm therefore, and do not submit again to a yoke of slavery. - Gal. 5.1 (ESV) (cf. Rom. 8.28-30; 1 Cor. 1.26-31; Eph. 1.18; 2 Thess. 2.13-14; Jude 1.1) **Faith** - "... for unless you believe that I am he you will die in your sins"... So Jesus said to the Jews who had believed in him, "If you abide in my word, you are truly my disciples, and you will know the truth, and the truth will set you free." - John 8.24b, 31-32 (ESV) (cf. Ps. 119.45; Rom. 1.17; 5.1-2; Eph. 2.8-9; 2 Tim. 1.13-14; Heb. 2.14-15; James 1.25) **Witness** - The Spirit of the Lord is upon me, because he has anointed me to proclaim good news to the poor. He has sent me to proclaim liberty to the captives and recovering of sight to the blind, to set at liberty those who are oppressed, to proclaim the year of the Lord's favor. - Luke 4.18-19 (ESV) (cf. Lev. 25.10; Prov. 31.8; Matt. 4.17; 28.18-20; Mark 13.10; Acts 1.8; 8.4, 12; 13.1-3; 25.20; 28.30-31)
Rev. 21.1-5 →	O, the depth of the riches and wisdom and knowledge of God! How unsearchable are his judgments, and how inscrutable his ways! For who has known the mind of the Lord, or who has been his counselor? Or who has ever given a gift to him, that he might be repaid?" For from him and through him and to him are all things. To him be glory forever! Amen! - Rom. 11.33-36(ESV) (cf. 1 Cor. 15.23-28; Rev.)	**Wholeness** (Sickness) But he was wounded for our transgressions; he was crushed for our iniquities; upon him was the chastisement that brought us peace, and with his stripes we are healed. - Isa. 53.5 (ESV)	*The Church is One Community Where the Sacraments are Rightly Administered, Therefore it is a Community of:* **Worship** - You shall serve the Lord your God, and he will bless your bread and your water, and I will take sickness away from among you. - Exod. 23.25 (ESV) (cf. Ps. 147.1-3; Heb. 12.28; Col. 3.16; Rev. 15.3-4; 19.5) **Covenant** - And the Holy Spirit also bears witness to us; for after the saying, "This is the covenant that I will make with them after those days, declares the Lord: I will put my laws on their hearts, and write them on their minds," then he adds, "I will remember their sins and their lawless deeds no more." - Heb. 10.15-17 (ESV) (cf. Isa. 54.10-17; Ezek. 34.25-31; 37.26-27; Mal. 2.4-5; Luke 22.20; 2 Cor. 3.6; Col. 3.15; Heb. 8.7-13; 12.22-24; 13.20-21) **Presence** - In him you also are being built together into a dwelling place for God by his Spirit. - Eph. 2.22 (ESV) (cf. Exod. 40.34-38; Ezek. 48.35; Matt. 18.18-20)
Isa. 11.6-9 →		**Justice** (Selfishness) Behold, my servant whom I have chosen, my beloved with whom my soul is well pleased. I will put my Spirit upon him, and he will proclaim justice to the Gentiles. He will not quarrel or cry aloud, nor will anyone hear his voice in the streets; a bruised reed he will not break, and a smoldering wick he will not quench, until he brings justice to victory.- Matt. 12.18-20(ESV)	*The Church is a Holy Community Where Discipline is Rightly Ordered, Therefore it is a Community of:* **Reconciliation** - For he himself is our peace, who has made us both one and has broken down in his flesh the dividing wall of hostility by abolishing the law of commandments and ordinances, that he might create in himself one new man in place of the two, so making peace, and might reconcile us both to God in one body through the cross, thereby killing the hostility. And he came and preached peace to you who were far off and peace to those who were near. For through him we both have access in one Spirit to the Father. - Eph. 2.14-18 (ESV) (cf. Exod. 23.4-9; Lev. 19.34; Deut. 10.18-19; Ezek. 22.29; Mic. 6.8; 2 Cor. 5.16-21) **Suffering** - Since therefore Christ suffered in the flesh, arm yourselves with the same way of thinking, for whoever has suffered in the flesh has ceased from sin, so as to live for the rest of the time in the flesh no longer for human passions but for the will of God. - 1 Pet. 4.1-2 (ESV) (cf. Luke 6.22; 10.3; Rom. 8.17; 2 Tim. 2.3; 3.12; 1 Pet. 2.20-24; Heb. 5.8; 13.11-14) **Service** - But Jesus called them to him and said, "You know that the rulers of the Gentiles lord it over them, and their great ones exercise authority over them. It shall not be so among you. But whoever would be great among you must be your servant, and whoever would be first among you must be your slave even as the Son of Man came not to be served but to serve, and to give his life as a ransom for many." - Matt. 20.25-28 (ESV) (cf. 1 John 4.16-18; Gal. 2.10)

APPENDIX 11

Living in the Already and the Not Yet Kingdom

Rev. Dr. Don L. Davis

The Spirit: The pledge of the inheritance (***arrabon***)

The Church: The foretaste (***aparche***) of the Kingdom

"In Christ": The rich life (***en Christos***) we share as citizens of the Kingdom

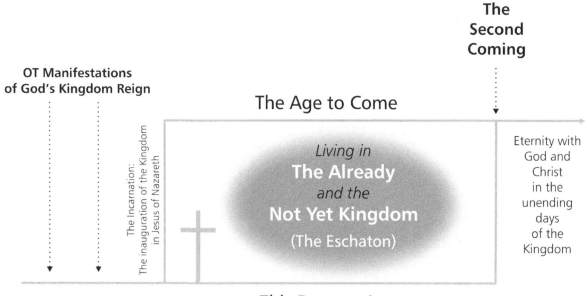

Internal enemy: The flesh (*sarx*) and the sin nature

External enemy: The world (*kosmos*) the systems of greed, lust, and pride

Infernal enemy: The devil (*kakos*) the animating spirit of falsehood and fear

Jewish View of Time

The Coming of Messiah

The restoration of Israel

The end of Gentile oppression

The return of the earth to Edenic glory

Universal knowledge of the Lord

APPENDIX 12

Jesus of Nazareth: The Presence of the Future

Rev. Dr. Don L. Davis

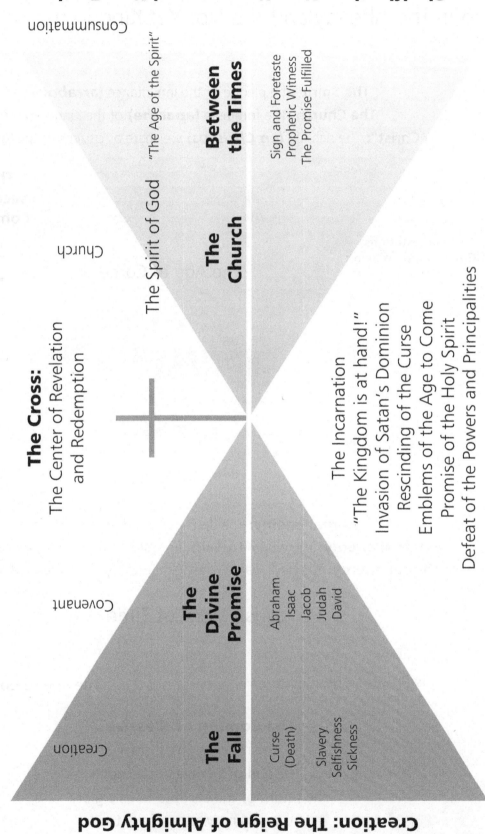

APPENDIX 13

Traditions
(Paradosis)
Dr. Don L. Davis and Rev. Terry G. Cornett

Strong's Definition

Paradosis. Transmission, i.e. (concretely) a precept; specifically, the Jewish traditionary law

Vine's Explanation

denotes "a tradition," and hence, by metonymy, (a) "the teachings of the rabbis," . . . (b) "apostolic teaching," . . . of instructions concerning the gatherings of believers, of Christian doctrine in general . . . of instructions concerning everyday conduct.

1. The concept of tradition in Scripture is essentially positive.

Jer. 6.16 (ESV) - Thus says the Lord: "Stand by the roads, and look, and ask for the ancient paths, where the good way is; and walk in it, and find rest for your souls. But they said, 'We will not walk in it'" (cf. Exod. 3.15; Judg. 2.17; 1 Kings 8.57-58; Ps. 78.1-6).

2 Chron. 35.25 (ESV) - Jeremiah also uttered a lament for Josiah; and all the singing men and singing women have spoken of Josiah in their laments to this day. They made these a rule in Israel; behold, they are written in the Laments (cf. Gen. 32.32; Judg. 11.38-40).

Jer. 35.14-19 (ESV) - The command that Jonadab the son of Rechab gave to his sons, to drink no wine, has been kept, and they drink none to this day, for they have obeyed their father's command. I have spoken to you persistently, but you have not listened to me. I have sent to you all my servants the prophets, sending them persistently, saying, 'Turn now every one of you from his evil way, and amend your deeds, and do not go after other gods to serve them, and then you shall dwell in the land that I gave to you and your fathers.' But you did not incline your ear or listen to me. The sons of Jonadab the son of Rechab have kept the command that their father gave them, but this people has not obeyed me. Therefore, thus says the

Traditions (continued)

Lord, the God of hosts, the God of Israel: Behold, I am bringing upon Judah and all the inhabitants of Jerusalem all the disaster that I have pronounced against them, because I have spoken to them and they have not listened, I have called to them and they have not answered." But to the house of the Rechabites Jeremiah said, "Thus says the Lord of hosts, the God of Israel: Because you have obeyed the command of Jonadab your father and kept all his precepts and done all that he commanded you, therefore thus says the Lord of hosts, the God of Israel: Jonadab the son of Rechab shall never lack a man to stand before me."

2. **Godly tradition is a wonderful thing, but not all tradition is godly.**

Any individual tradition must be judged by its faithfulness to the Word of God and its usefulness in helping people maintain obedience to Christ's example and teaching.[1] In the Gospels, Jesus frequently rebukes the Pharisees for establishing traditions that nullify rather than uphold God's commands.

Mark 7.8 (ESV) - You leave the commandment of God and hold to the tradition of men" (cf. Matt. 15.2-6; Mark 7.13).

Col. 2.8 (ESV) - See to it that no one takes you captive by philosophy and empty deceit, according to human tradition, according to the elemental spirits of the world, and not according to Christ.

3. **Without the fullness of the Holy Spirit, and the constant edification provided to us by the Word of God, tradition will inevitably lead to dead formalism.**

Those who are spiritual are filled with the Holy Spirit, whose power and leading alone provides individuals and congregations a sense of freedom and vitality in all they practice and believe. However, when the practices and teachings of any given tradition are no longer infused by the power of the Holy Spirit and the Word of God, tradition loses its effectiveness, and may actually become counterproductive to our discipleship in Jesus Christ.

Eph. 5.18 (ESV) - And do not get drunk with wine, for that is debauchery, but be filled with the Spirit.

[1] *"All Protestants insist that these traditions must ever be tested against Scripture and can never possess an independent apostolic authority over or alongside of Scripture." (J. Van Engen, "Tradition,"* **Evangelical Dictionary of Theology,** *Walter Elwell, Gen. ed.) We would add that Scripture is itself the "authoritative tradition" by which all other traditions are judged. See "Appendix A, The Founders of Tradition: Three Levels of Christian Authority," p. 4.*

Gal. 5.22-25 (ESV) - But the fruit of the Spirit is love, joy, peace, patience, kindness, goodness, faithfulness, gentleness, self-control; against such things there is no law. And those who belong to Christ Jesus have crucified the flesh with its passions and desires. If we live by the Spirit, let us also walk by the Spirit.

2 Cor. 3.5-6 (ESV) - Not that we are sufficient in ourselves to claim anything as coming from us, but our sufficiency is from God, who has made us competent to be ministers of a new covenant, not of the letter but of the Spirit. For the letter kills, but the Spirit gives life.

4. **Fidelity to the Apostolic Tradition (teaching and modeling) is the essence of Christian maturity.**

2 Tim. 2.2 (ESV) - and what you have heard from me in the presence of many witnesses entrust to faithful men who will be able to teach others also.

1 Cor. 11.1-2 (ESV) - Be imitators of me, as I am of Christ. Now I commend you because you remember me in everything and maintain the traditions even as I delivered them to you (cf.1 Cor. 4.16-17, 2 Tim. 1.13-14, 2 Thess. 3.7-9, Phil. 4.9).

1 Cor. 15.3-8 (ESV) - For I delivered to you as of first importance what I also received: that Christ died for our sins in accordance with the Scriptures, that he was buried, that he was raised on the third day in accordance with the Scriptures, and that he appeared to Cephas, then to the twelve. Then he appeared to more than five hundred brothers at one time, most of whom are still alive, though some have fallen asleep. Then he appeared to James, then to all the apostles. Last of all, as to one untimely born, he appeared also to me.

5. **The Apostle Paul often includes an appeal to the tradition for support in doctrinal practices.**

1 Cor. 11.16 (ESV) - If anyone is inclined to be contentious, we have no such practice, nor do the churches of God (cf. 1 Cor. 1.2, 7.17, 15.3).

Traditions (continued)

> 1 Cor. 14.33-34 (ESV) - For God is not a God of confusion but of peace. As in all the churches of the saints, the women should keep silent in the churches. For they are not permitted to speak, but should be in submission, as the Law also says.

6. When a congregation uses received tradition to remain faithful to the "Word of God," they are commended by the apostles.

> 1 Cor. 11.2 (ESV) - Now I commend you because you remember me in everything and maintain the traditions even as I delivered them to you.

> 2 Thess. 2.15 (ESV) - So then, brothers, stand firm and hold to the traditions that you were taught by us, either by our spoken word or by our letter.

> 2 Thess. 3.6 (ESV) - Now we command you, brothers, in the name of our Lord Jesus Christ, that you keep away from any brother who is walking in idleness and not in accord with the tradition that you received from us.

Appendix A

The Founders of Tradition: Three Levels of Christian Authority

Exod. 3.15 (ESV) - God also said to Moses, "Say this to the people of Israel, 'The Lord, the God of your fathers, the God of Abraham, the God of Isaac, and the God of Jacob, has sent me to you.' This is my name forever, and thus I am to be remembered throughout all generations."

1. The Authoritative Tradition: the Apostles and the Prophets (The Holy Scriptures)

Eph. 2.19-21 (ESV) - So then you are no longer strangers and aliens, but you are fellow citizens with the saints and members of the household of God, built on the foundation of the apostles and prophets, Christ Jesus himself being the cornerstone, in whom the whole structure, being joined together, grows into a holy temple in the Lord.

~ The Apostle Paul

Those who gave eyewitness testimony to the revelation and saving acts of Yahweh, first in Israel, and ultimately in Jesus Christ the Messiah. This testimony is binding for all people, at all times, and in all places. It is the authoritative tradition by which all subsequent tradition is judged.

2. The Great Tradition: the Ecumenical Councils and their Creeds[2]

What has been believed everywhere, always, and by all.

~ Vincent of Lerins

The Great Tradition is the core dogma (doctrine) of the Church. It represents the teaching of the Church as it has understood the Authoritative Tradition (the Holy Scriptures), and summarizes those essential truths that Christians of all ages have confessed and believed. To these doctrinal statements the whole Church, (Catholic, Orthodox, and Protestant)[3] gives its assent. The worship and theology of the Church reflects this core dogma, which finds its summation and fulfillment in the person and work of Jesus Christ. From earliest times, Christians have expressed their devotion to God in its Church calendar, a yearly pattern of worship which summarizes and reenacts the events of Christ's life.

3. Specific Church Traditions: the Founders of Denominations and Orders

The Presbyterian Church (U.S.A.) has approximately 2.5 million members, 11,200 congregations and 21,000 ordained ministers. Presbyterians trace their history to the 16th century and the Protestant Reformation. Our heritage, and much of what we believe, began with the French lawyer John Calvin (1509-1564), whose writings crystallized much of the Reformed thinking that came before him.

~ The Presbyterian Church, U.S.A.

Christians have expressed their faith in Jesus Christ in various ways through specific movements and traditions which embrace and express the Authoritative Tradition and the Great Tradition in unique ways. For instance,

[2] See Appendix B, "Defining the Great Tradition."

[3] Even the more radical wing of the Protestant reformation (Anabaptists) who were the most reluctant to embrace the creeds as dogmatic instruments of faith, did not disagree with the essential content found in them. "They assumed the Apostolic Creed–they called it 'The Faith,' *Der Glaube*, as did most people." See John Howard Yoder, *Preface to Theology: Christology and Theological Method.* Grand Rapids: Brazos Press, 2002. pp. 222-223.

Traditions (continued)

Catholic movements have arisen around people like Benedict, Francis, or Dominic, and among Protestants people like Martin Luther, John Calvin, Ulrich Zwingli, and John Wesley. Women have founded vital movements of Christian faith (e.g., Aimee Semple McPherson of the Foursquare Church), as well as minorities (e.g., Richard Allen of the African Methodist Episcopal Church or Charles H. Mason of the Church of God in Christ, who also helped to spawn the Assemblies of God), all which attempted to express the Authoritative Tradition and the Great Tradition in a specific way consistent with their time and expression.

The emergence of vital, dynamic movements of the faith at different times and among different peoples reveal the fresh working of the Holy Spirit throughout history. Thus, inside Catholicism, new communities have arisen such as the Benedictines, Franciscans, and Dominicans; and outside Catholicism, new denominations have emerged (Lutherans, Presbyterians, Methodists, Church of God in Christ, etc.). Each of these specific traditions have "founders," key leaders whose energy and vision helped to establish a unique expression of Christian faith and practice. Of course, to be legitimate, these movements must adhere to and faithfully express both the Authoritative Tradition and the Great Tradition. Members of these specific traditions embrace their own unique practices and patterns of spirituality, but these unique features are not necessarily binding on the Church at large. They represent the unique expressions of that community's understanding of and faithfulness to the Authoritative and Great Traditions.

Specific traditions seek to express and live out this faithfulness to the Authoritative and Great Traditions through their worship, teaching, and service. They seek to make the Gospel clear within new cultures or sub-cultures, speaking and modeling the hope of Christ into new situations shaped by their own set of questions posed in light of their own unique circumstances. These movements, therefore, seek to contextualize the Authoritative tradition in a way that faithfully and effectively leads new groups of people to faith in Jesus Christ, and incorporates those who believe into the community of faith that obeys his teachings and gives witness of him to others.

Appendix B

Defining the "Great Tradition"

The Great Tradition (sometimes called the "classical Christian tradition") is defined by Robert E. Webber as follows:

> *[It is] the broad outline of Christian belief and practice developed from the Scriptures between the time of Christ and the middle of the fifth century*
>
> ~ Webber. **The Majestic Tapestry**.
> Nashville: Thomas Nelson Publishers, 1986. p. 10.

This tradition is widely affirmed by Protestant theologians both ancient and modern.

> *Thus those ancient Councils of Nicea, Constantinople, the first of Ephesus, Chalcedon, and the like, which were held for refuting errors, we willingly embrace, and reverence as sacred, in so far as relates to doctrines of faith, for they contain nothing but the pure and genuine interpretation of Scripture, which the holy Fathers with spiritual prudence adopted to crush the enemies of religion who had then arisen.*
>
> ~ John Calvin. **Institutes**. IV, ix. 8.

> *. . . most of what is enduringly valuable in contemporary biblical exegesis was discovered by the fifth century.*
>
> ~ Thomas C. Oden. **The Word of Life**.
> San Francisco: HarperSanFrancisco, 1989. p. xi

> *The first four Councils are by far the most important, as they settled the orthodox faith on the Trinity and the Incarnation.*
>
> ~ Philip Schaff. **The Creeds of Christendom**. Vol. 1.
> Grand Rapids: Baker Book House, 1996. p. 44.

Our reference to the Ecumenical Councils and Creeds is, therefore, focused on those Councils which retain a widespread agreement in the Church among Catholics, Orthodox, and Protestants. While Catholic and Orthodox share common agreement on the first seven councils, Protestants tend to affirm and use primarily the first four. Therefore, those councils which continue to be shared by the whole Church are completed with the Council of Chalcedon in 451.

Traditions (continued)

It is worth noting that each of these four Ecumenical Councils took place in a pre-European cultural context and that none of them were held in Europe. They were councils of the whole Church and they reflected a time in which Christianity was primarily an eastern religion in it's geographic core. By modern reckoning, their participants were African, Asian, and European. The councils reflected a church that ". . . has roots in cultures far distant from Europe and preceded the development of modern European identity, and [of which] some of its greatest minds have been African" (Oden, *The Living God*, San Francisco: HarperSanFrancisco, 1987, p. 9).

Perhaps the most important achievement of the Councils was the creation of what is now commonly called the Nicene Creed. It serves as a summary statement of the Christian faith that can be agreed on by Catholic, Orthodox, and Protestant Christians.

The first four Ecumenical Councils are summarized in the following chart:

Name/Date/Location	Purpose
First Ecumenical Council 325 A.D. *Nicea, Asia Minor*	Defending against: *Arianism* Question answered: *Was Jesus God?* Action: *Developed the initial form of the Nicene Creed to serve as a summary of the Christian faith*
Second Ecumenical Council 381 A.D. *Constantinople, Asia Minor*	Defending against: *Macedonianism* Question answered: *Is the Holy Spirit a personal and equal part of the Godhead?* Action: *Completed the Nicene Creed by expanding the article dealing with the Holy Spirit*
Third Ecumenical Council 431 A.D. *Ephesus, Asia Minor*	Defending against: *Nestorianism* Question answered: *Is Jesus Christ both God and man in one person?* Action: *Defined Christ as the Incarnate Word of God and affirmed his mother Mary as* **theotokos** *(God-bearer)*
Fourth Ecumenical Council 451 A.D. *Chalcedon, Asia Minor*	Defending against: *Monophysitism* Question answered: *How can Jesus be both God and man?* Action: *Explained the relationship between Jesus' two natures (human and Divine)*

APPENDIX 14

St. Basil, the Nicene Creed, and the Doctrine of the Holy Spirit

Rev. Terry G. Cornett

[1] *Basil was born in 329, in the region of Pontus (now modern day Turkey), to a wealthy and rather remarkable family. His grandfather, his father, his mother, his sister and his two younger brothers were all eventually named as saints by the Church. He received an outstanding education at schools in Caesarea, Constantinople, and Athens. Following his education Basil became first a monk in Pontus, then a presbyter (a pastoral position) at Caesarea (where he eventually became a bishop) and developed into a vigorous theologian as well. In these roles, he developed a reputation for personal integrity and great compassion. Even as a bishop he owned only one undergarment and one outer garment and did not eat meat at his table. He lived simply, treated his body harshly, and was personally involved with the distribution to the poor. Because of his personal integrity his many theological opponents through the years had difficulty finding anything wrong to charge him with.*

The original Nicene Creed came out the first worldwide gathering of Christian leaders at Nicea in Bithynia (what is now Isnik, Turkey) in the year 325. It was called to deal with a heresy called Arianism which denied that Jesus was God and taught that he was instead the greatest created being. The council at Nicaea, condemned Arianism, and hammered out language that the bishops could use to teach their churches who Jesus truly was.

A little over 50 years later, however, additional challenges were being faced by the Church. A modified form of the Arian heresy was making a comeback; Macedonius, an Arian theologian, had been elected as Bishop of Constantinople in 341. A new problem had also emerged: some Christian bishops had begun teaching that the Holy Spirit was not God. Macedonius eventually became the leader of the sect of Pneumatomachi, whose distinctive tenet was that the Holy Spirit is not God but rather a created being similar to the angels. They taught that the Holy Spirit is subordinate to the Father and the Son and functions as their servant.

Basil[1] is one of the key ancient theologians who communicated and defended the biblical doctrine of the Holy Spirit against these heresies. Basil was a bishop of Caesarea who lived in the 4th century A.D. He wrote *De Spiritu Sancto* ("On the Holy Spirit") in 374 just a few years before his death in 379. This book defended the belief that the Holy Spirit is God. Basil worked tirelessly to see that a new Church council would be called to affirm this doctrine and see that it was taught in the churches.

In 381, shortly after Basil's death, a council of 150 bishops of the Eastern Church were gathered in Constantinople (modern day Istanbul, Turkey). This council reaffirmed the fact that Jesus was fully God and then turned their attention to the question of the Holy Spirit which the Nicene council had left untouched. (The original Nicene Creed read simply, "We believe in the Holy Spirit"). Building on Basil's writings, the council turned this simple statement into a paragraph which explained more fully the person and work of the Holy Spirit.

St. Basil, the Nicene Creed, and the Doctrine of the Holy Spirit (continued)

This amended version of the original Nicene Creed (technically the Nicene-Constantinopolitan Creed) is commonly referred to simply as the "Nicene Creed" since it is the final version of the statement started at Nicea. It is accepted by Catholics, Orthodox[2], and Protestant Christians alike as the summary of scriptural teaching which separates orthodoxy from heresy.

[2] *Although the Orthodox do not include the phrase "and the Son" (which was added at a later date) in the statement about the Spirit proceeding from the Father.*

APPENDIX 15

The Father, Son, and Holy Ghost
Share the Same Divine Attributes and Works
Supporting Scriptures
Adapted from Edward Henry Bickersteth, **The Trinity**. *Grand Rapids: Kregel Publications, 1957. Rpt. 1980.*

Attribute of God	God the Father	God the Son	God the Holy Spirit
God Is Eternal (Deut. 33.27)	Isa. 44.6; Rom. 16.26	John 8.58; Rev. 1.17-18	Heb. 9.14
God Created All Things (Rev. 4.11) and Is the Source of Life (Deut. 30.20)	Pss. 36.9; 100.3; 1 Cor. 8.6	John 1.3, 4; Col. 1.16	Gen. 1.2; Pss. 33.6; 104.30; Job 33.4; John 7.38-39; Rom. 8.11
God Is Incomprehensible (1 Tim. 6.16) and Omniscient (Jer. 16.17)	Isa. 46.9-10; Matt. 11.27; Heb. 4.13	Matt. 11.27; John 21.17	Isa. 40.13-14; 1 Cor. 2.10; John 16.15
God Is Omnipresent (Jer. 23.24)	Acts 17.27-28	Matt. 18.20; 28.20	Ps. 139.7-10
God Is Omnipotent (2 Chron. 20.6) and Sovereignly Acts as He Chooses (Job 42.2)	Luke 1.37; Eph. 1.11	John 14.14; Matt. 11.27	Zech. 4.6; Rom. 15.19; 1 Cor. 12.11
God Is True, Holy, Righteous, and Good (Ps. 119)	Ps. 34.8; John 7.28; 17.11, 25	John 14.6; 10.11; Acts 3.14	1 John 5.6; John 14.26; Ps. 143.10
God is the Source of Strength for His People (Exod. 15.2)	Ps. 18.32	Phil. 4.13	Eph. 3.16
God Alone Forgives and Cleanses from Sin (Pss. 51.7; 130.3-4)	Exod. 34.6-7	Mark 2.7-11	1 Cor. 6.11; Heb. 9.14

The Father, Son, and Holy Ghost Share the Same Divine Attributes and Works (continued)

Attribute of God	God the Father	God the Son	God the Holy Spirit
God Gave Humanity the Divine Law Which Revealed His Character and Will (2 Tim. 3.16)	Ezek. 2.4; Isa. 40.8; Deut. 9.10	Matt. 24.35; John 5.39; Heb. 1.1-2	2 Sam. 23.2; 2 Pet. 1.21; Rom. 8.2
God Dwells in and among the People Who Believe in Him (Isa. 57.15)	2 Cor. 6.16; 1 Cor. 14.25	Eph. 3.17; Matt. 18.20	John 14.17; 1 Cor. 6.19; Eph. 2.22
God Is the Supreme, Highest Being Who Has No Equal, Who Reigns as Lord and King over All Creation, and Who Alone Is to Be Worshiped and Glorified	Isa. 42.8; Ps. 47.2; 1 Tim. 6.15; Matt. 4.10; Rev. 22.8-9	John 20.28-29; Rev. 17.14; Heb. 1.3, 6-8	Matt. 12.31; Luke 1.35; 2 Cor. 3.18; 1 Pet. 4.14; John 4.24

APPENDIX 16

Examples of Denominational Statements on "Baptism in the Holy Spirit" Which Illustrate the Differing Views

Single Stage View

Evangelical Presbyterian Church

Excerpted from Position Paper on the Holy Spirit, www.epc.org/about-epc/position-papers/holy-spirit.html

As a denomination in the Reformed tradition, we subscribe to the ancient affirmation of orthodox Christian faith and believe in "one Lord, one faith, one baptism" (Ephesians 4:5). This baptism, while visibly expressed in the covenant sacrament that bears its name is invisibly the work of the Spirit that takes place at the time of the new birth. Paul expresses this truth in I Corinthians 12:13, when he tells the Corinthians "...we were all baptized by one Spirit into one body..."

Thus, we hold to the concept of the baptism in or with the Holy Spirit as the act of the Spirit that takes an unregenerate individual and, through the new birth, adopts him into the family of God. All the works of the Spirit that follow, then, are because of this initial baptism rather than separate from it.

Since Christians are called to "...be filled with the Spirit..." (Ephesians 5:18) all believers in Christ having been baptized into His body by the Holy Spirit should seek to experience the fulfillment of this command. We believe that Christians are called upon to proclaim a grace that reaches out to forgive, to redeem and to give new spiritual power to life through Jesus Christ and the infilling of the Holy Spirit." (*Book of Worship*, 1-3).

Multiple Stage View: Holiness

Church of the Nazarene

Excerpted from Articles of Faith, www.nazarene.org/gensec/we_believe.html

We believe that entire sanctification is that act of God, subsequent to regeneration, by which believers are made free from original sin, or depravity, and brought into a state of entire devotement to God, and the holy obedience of love made perfect.

It is wrought by the baptism with the Holy Spirit, and comprehends in one experience the cleansing of the heart from sin and the abiding, indwelling presence of the Holy Spirit, empowering the believer for life and service.

Entire sanctification is provided by the blood of Jesus, is wrought instantaneously by faith, preceded by entire consecration; and to this work and state of grace the Holy Spirit bears witness.

This experience is also known by various terms representing its different phases, such as "Christian perfection," "perfect love," "heart purity," "the baptism with the Holy Spirit," "the fullness of the blessing," and "Christian holiness."

We believe that there is a marked distinction between a pure heart and a mature character. The former is obtained in an instant, the result of entire sanctification; the latter is the result of growth in grace.

We believe that the grace of entire sanctification includes the impulse to grow in grace. However, this impulse must be consciously nurtured, and careful attention given to the requisites and processes of spiritual development and improvement in Christlikeness of character and personality. Without such purposeful endeavor one's witness may be impaired and the grace itself frustrated and ultimately lost.

Assemblies of God

Excerpted from The Initial Physical Evidence of the Baptism in the Holy Spirit, http://ag.org/top/position_papers/0000_index.cfm

Multiple Stage View: Pentecostal

The term baptism in the Holy Spirit is taken from Scripture. John the Baptist was the first to use it shortly before Jesus began His public ministry. He said, "He [Jesus] shall baptize you with the Holy Ghost" (Matthew 3:11). At the conclusion of His earthly ministry, Jesus referred to John's statement (Acts 1:5); and Peter, in reporting on the events in the home of Cornelius, also repeated the statement (Acts 11:16).

The baptism in the Spirit (also referred to herein as the Baptism) is subsequent to and distinct from the new birth. Scripture makes it clear there is an experience in which the Holy Spirit baptizes believers into the body of Christ (1 Corinthians 12:13), and there is the experience in which Christ baptizes believers in the Holy Spirit (Matthew 3:11). These cannot refer to the same experience since the agent who does the baptizing and the element into which the candidate is baptized are different in each case.

The distinctiveness of the experiences is illustrated in several places. The case of the Ephesian disciples is an example. After they stated they had experienced only John's baptism (Acts 19:3), Paul explained they were to believe on Christ Jesus. Then these disciples were baptized in water, after which Paul laid hands on them and the Holy Spirit came on them. The lapse of time was brief between these disciples' believing on Christ and the Holy Spirit's coming upon them, but it was long enough for them to be baptized in water. The baptism in the Spirit was distinct from and subsequent to salvation.

The baptism in the Spirit is not an end in itself, but a means to an end. The scriptural ideal for the believer is to be continually filled with the Spirit. The Baptism is the crisis experience which introduces the believer to the process experience of living a Spirit-filled life.

The expression initial physical evidence of the Baptism refers to the first outward sign that the Holy Spirit has come in filling power. A study of Scripture indicates there was a physical sign by which observers knew that believers had been baptized in the Holy Spirit. The evidence always occurred at the very time the believers were baptized in the Spirit and not on some future occasion.

In the home of Cornelius there was convincing evidence of the Holy Spirit being poured out on the Gentiles (Acts 10:44-48). Later, when Peter was called upon to explain to the leaders of the church in Jerusalem his ministry in the home of Cornelius, he referred to observable evidence of the believers being baptized in the Holy Spirit. He cited this as the reason why he arranged for the believers to be baptized in water (Acts 11:15-17).

While speaking in tongues has initial evidential value, it is designed by God to be much more than evidence of a past experience. It also continues to bring enrichment to the individual believer in personal devotions, and to the congregation when accompanied by the interpretation of tongues.

Combination View:
Pentecostal-Holiness

Church of God in Christ

Excerpted from The Doctrines of the Church of God in Christ, http://www.cogic.org/doctrnes.htm

We believe that the Baptism of the Holy Ghost is an experience subsequent to conversion and sanctification and that tongue-speaking is the consequence of the baptism in the Holy Ghost with the manifestations of the fruit of the spirit (Galatians 5:22-23; Acts 10:46, 19:1-6). We believe that we are not baptized with the Holy Ghost in order to be saved (Acts 19:1-6; John 3:5). When one receives a baptismal Holy Ghost experience, we believe one will speak with a tongue unknown to oneself according to the sovereign will of Christ. To be filled with the Spirit means to be Spirit controlled as expressed by Paul in Ephesians 5:18-19. Since the charismatic demonstrations were necessary to help the early church to be successful in implementing the command of Christ, we therefore, believe that a Holy Ghost experience is mandatory for all men today.

Association of Vineyard Churches

Excerpted from Vineyard Statement of Faith,
www.vineyardusa.org/about/beliefs/beliefs_index/faith/paragraph_07.htm

**Combination View:
Charismatic**

WE BELIEVE that the Holy Spirit was poured out on the Church at Pentecost in power, baptizing believers into the Body of Christ and releasing the gifts of the Spirit to them. The Spirit brings the permanent indwelling presence of God to us for spiritual worship, personal sanctification, building up the Church, gifting us for ministry, and driving back the kingdom of Satan by the evangelization of the world through proclaiming the word of Jesus and doing the works of Jesus.

WE BELIEVE that the Holy Spirit indwells every believer in Jesus Christ and that He is our abiding Helper, Teacher, and Guide. We believe in the filling or empowering of the Holy Spirit, often a conscious experience, for ministry today. We believe in the present ministry of the Spirit and in the exercise of all of the biblical gifts of the Spirit. We practice the laying on of hands for the empowering of the Spirit, for healing, and for recognition and empowering of those whom God has ordained to lead and serve the Church.

APPENDIX 17

The Key Passages on Spiritual Gifts in the New Testament

Romans 12.3-12 (ESV)

For by the grace given to me I say to everyone among you not to think of himself more highly than he ought to think, but to think with sober judgment, each according to the measure of faith that God has assigned. [4] For as in one body we have many members, and the members do not all have the same function, [5] so we, though many, are one body in Christ, and individually members one of another. [6] Having gifts that differ according to the grace given to us, let us use them: if prophecy, in proportion to our faith; [7] if service, in our serving; the one who teaches, in his teaching; [8] the one who exhorts, in his exhortation; the one who contributes, in generosity; the one who leads, with zeal; the one who does acts of mercy, with cheerfulness. [9] Let love be genuine. Abhor what is evil; hold fast to what is good. [10] Love one another with brotherly affection. Outdo one another in showing honor. [11] Do not be slothful in zeal, be fervent in spirit, serve the Lord. [12] Rejoice in hope, be patient in tribulation, be constant in prayer.

1 Corinthians 12.1-31a (ESV)

Now concerning spiritual gifts, brothers, I do not want you to be uninformed. [2] You know that when you were pagans you were led astray to mute idols, however you were led. [3] Therefore I want you to understand that no one speaking in the Spirit of God ever says "Jesus is accursed!" and no one can say "Jesus is Lord" except in the Holy Spirit. [4] Now there are varieties of gifts, but the same Spirit; [5] and there are varieties of service, but the same Lord; [6] and there are varieties of activities, but it is the same God who empowers them all in everyone. [7] To each is given the manifestation of the Spirit for the common good. [8] To one is given through the Spirit the utterance of wisdom, and to another the utterance of knowledge according to the same Spirit, [9] to another faith by the same Spirit, to another gifts of healing by the one Spirit, [10] to another the working of miracles, to another prophecy, to another the ability to distinguish between spirits, to another various kinds of tongues, to another the interpretation of tongues. [11] All these are empowered by one and the same Spirit, who apportions to each one individually as he wills. [12] For just as the body is one and has many members, and all the members of the body, though many, are one body, so it is with Christ. [13] For in one Spirit we were all baptized into one body— Jews or Greeks, slaves or free—and all were made to drink of one Spirit. [14] For the body does not consist of one member but of many. [15] If the foot should say, "Because I am not a hand, I do not belong to the body," that would not make it any less a part of the body. [16] And if the ear should say, "Because I am not an eye, I do not belong to the body," that would not make it any less a part of the body. [17] If the whole body were an eye, where would be the sense of hearing? If the whole body were an ear, where would be the sense of smell? [18] But as it is, God arranged the members in the body, each one of them, as he chose. [19] If all were a single member, where would the body be? [20] As it is, there are many parts, yet one body. [21] The eye cannot say to the hand, "I have no need of you," nor again the head to the feet, "I have no need of you." [22] On the contrary, the parts of the body that seem to be weaker are indispensable, [23] and on those parts of the body that we think less honorable we bestow the greater honor, and our unpresentable parts are treated with greater modesty, [24] which our more presentable parts do not require. But God has so composed the body, giving greater honor to the part that lacked it, [25] that there may be no division in the body, but that the members may have the same care for one another. [26] If one member suffers, all suffer together; if one member is honored, all rejoice together. [27] Now you are the body of Christ and individually members of it. [28] And God has appointed in the church first apostles, second prophets, third teachers, then miracles, then gifts of healing, helping, administrating, and various kinds of tongues. [29] Are all apostles? Are all prophets? Are all teachers? Do all work miracles? [30] Do all possess gifts of healing? Do all speak with tongues? Do all interpret? [31] But earnestly desire the higher gifts (cf. 1 Cor. 14.1-40).

Ephesians 4.7-16 (ESV)

But grace was given to each one of us according to the measure of Christ's gift. [8] Therefore it says, "When he ascended on high he led a host of captives, and he gave gifts to men." [9] (In saying, "He ascended," what does it mean but that he had also descended into the lower parts of the earth? [10] He who descended is the one who also ascended far above all the heavens, that he might fill all things.) [11] And he gave the apostles, the prophets, the evangelists, the pastors and teachers, [12] to equip the saints for the work of ministry, for building up the body of Christ, [13] until we all attain to the unity of the faith and of the knowledge of the Son of God, to mature manhood, to the measure of the stature of the fullness of Christ, [14] so that we may no longer be children, tossed to and fro by the waves and carried about by every wind of doctrine, by human cunning, by craftiness in deceitful schemes. [15] Rather, speaking the truth in love, we are to grow up in every way into him who is the head, into Christ, [16] from whom the whole body, joined and held together by every joint with which it is equipped, when each part is working properly, makes the body grow so that it builds itself up in love.

1 Peter 4.7-11 (ESV)

The end of all things is at hand; therefore be self-controlled and sober-minded for the sake of your prayers. [8] Above all, keep loving one another earnestly, since love covers a multitude of sins. [9] Show hospitality to one another without grumbling. [10] As each has received a gift, use it to serve one another, as good stewards of God's varied grace: [11] whoever speaks, as one who speaks oracles of God; whoever serves, as one who serves by the strength that God supplies—in order that in everything God may be glorified through Jesus Christ. To him belong glory and dominion forever and ever. Amen.

APPENDIX 18

Spiritual Gifts Specifically Mentioned in the New Testament

Rev. Terry G. Cornett

Administration	1 Cor. 12.28	The ability to bring order to Church life.
Apostleship	1 Cor. 12.28; Eph. 4.11	The ability to establish new churches among the unreached, nurture them to maturity, and exercise the authority and wisdom necessary to see them permanently established and able to reproduce; and/or A gift unique to the founding of the Church age which included the reception of special revelation and uniquely binding leadership authority
Discernment	1 Cor. 12.10	The ability to serve the Church through a Spirit-given ability to distinguish between God's truth (his presence, working, and doctrine) and fleshly error or satanic counterfeits
Evangelism	Eph. 4.11	The passion and the ability to effectively proclaim the Gospel so that people understand it
Exhortation	Rom. 12.8	The ability to give encouragement or rebuke that helps others obey Christ
Faith	1 Cor. 12.9	The ability to build up the Church through a unique ability to see the unrealized purposes of God and unwaveringly trust God to accomplish them
Giving	Rom. 12.8	The ability to build up a church through taking delight in the consistent, generous sharing of spiritual and physical resources
Healing	1 Cor. 12.9; 12.28	The ability to exercise faith that results in restoring people to physical, emotional, and spiritual health
Interpretation	1 Cor. 12.10	The ability to explain the meaning of an ecstatic utterance so that the Church is edified
Knowledge	1 Cor. 12.8	The ability to understand scriptural truth, through the illumination of the Holy Spirit, and speak it out to edify the body; and/or The supernatural revelation of the existence, or nature, of a person or thing which would not be known through natural means

Spiritual Gifts Specifically Mentioned in the New Testament (continued)

Leadership	Rom. 12.8	Spiritually-inspired courage, wisdom, zeal, and hard work which motivates and guides others so that they can effectively participate in building the Church
Mercy	Rom. 12.8	Sympathy of heart which enables a person to empathize with and cheerfully serve those who are sick, hurting, or discouraged
Ministering (or Service, or Helping, or Hospitality)	Rom. 12.7; 1 Pet. 4.9	The ability to joyfully perform any task which benefits others and meets their practical and material needs (especially on behalf of the poor or afflicted)
Miracles	1 Cor. 12.10; 12.28	The ability to confront evil and do good in ways that make visible the awesome power and presence of God
Pastoring	Eph. 4.11	The desire and ability to guide, protect, and equip the members of a congregation for ministry
Prophecy	1 Cor. 12.28; Rom. 12.6	The ability to receive and proclaim openly a revealed message from God which prepares the Church for obedience to him and to the Scriptures
Teaching	1 Cor. 12.28; Rom. 12.7; Eph. 4.11	The ability to explain the meaning of the Word of God and its application through careful instruction
Tongues	1 Cor. 12.10; 12.28	Ecstatic utterance by which a person speaks to God (or others) under the direction of the Holy Spirit
Wisdom	1 Cor. 12.8	Spirit-revealed insight that allows a person to speak godly instruction for solving problems; and/or Spirit-revealed insight that allows a person to explain the central mysteries of the Christian faith

APPENDIX 19

Areas of Disagreement among Christians Concerning Spiritual Gifts

Rev. Terry G. Cornett

I. What Is the Relationship between "Natural Talents or Capacities" and "Spiritual Gifts"?

A. View #1 - Spiritual gifts are what the natural talents and abilities latent in every human being look like when they are energized, empowered, broadened, and redirected by the Spirit of God regenerating a person.

This view is concerned to safeguard the fact that:

1. There is no discontinuity between the activity of the Spirit who creates and who recreates. (Salvation is restorative in nature making us the full human beings we were originally created to be.)

2. That God has chosen to work his gifts through human beings which includes using their minds, bodies, and personalities. He includes us in his work so that even though his power will enable us to do far more than mere human accomplishments, it is still at work in, with, and through us as we actually are.

3. God foreknew us and was at work prior to our salvation (cf. Jer. 1.5)

   a. Jer. 1.5 (ESV) - Before I formed you in the womb I knew you, and before you were born I consecrated you; I appointed you a prophet to the nations.

   b. Eph. 2.10 (ESV) - For we are his workmanship, created in Christ Jesus for good works, which God prepared beforehand, that we should walk in them.

Areas of Disagreement among Christians Concerning Spiritual Gifts (continued)

4. That even those who are unsaved and in rebellion against God rely on his creation and gifts of grace (suppressed, corrupted, or misdirected as they may be) for their very being and productivity.

   a. 1 Cor. 4.7 (ESV) - For who sees anything different in you? What do you have that you did not receive? If then you received it, why do you boast as if you did not receive it? (Cf. Ps. 104.)

   b. Matt. 5.45 (ESV) - . . . so that you may be sons of your Father who is in heaven. For he makes his sun rise on the evil and on the good, and sends rain on the just and on the unjust.

   c. "The same God is God of creation and of new creation, working out both through his perfect will. . . . God's gracious purpose for each of us is eternal. It was formed and even "given" to us in Christ "before eternal time" (2 Tim. 1.9, literally); God chose us to be holy and destined us to be his sons through Jesus Christ "before the foundation of the world" (Eph. 1.4,5); and the good works for which were re-created in Christ are precisely those "which God prepared beforehand." This fundamental truth that God planned the end from the beginning should warn us against . . . [too easily separating] . . . between nature and grace, between our pre-conversion and our post-conversion life" (John R. W. Stott, *Baptism and Fullness: The Work of the Holy Spirit Today*).

B. View #2 - Spiritual gifts are new supernatural abilities given to Christians which are only available to us through God's power and are able to accomplish things far beyond the reach of human ability.

This view is concerned to safeguard the fact that:

1. Salvation is transformative as well as restorative.

2. God is able to supply whatever is needed in a situation regardless of the resources we seem to have available. We are dependent upon God's Spirit, not our own resources.

3. Supernatural powers exceeding anything possible in the natural order are available to the body of Christ.

4. We all are commanded to seek certain spiritual gifts that are of benefit to the body (1 Cor. 12.31 & 14.12). The gifts are always spoken of in relation to how they build up Christ's body. There is no scriptural reference to spiritual gifts apart from their use in and by the Church.

   a. 1 Cor. 1.26-29 (ESV) - For consider your calling, brothers: not many of you were wise according to worldly standards, not many were powerful, not many were of noble birth. [27] But God chose what is foolish in the world to shame the wise; God chose what is weak in the world to shame the strong; [28] God chose what is low and despised in the world, even things that are not, to bring to nothing things that are, [29] so that no human being might boast in the presence of God.

   b. Non-Christians have talents through common grace. . . but these are talents, not gifts. No unbeliever has a spiritual gift. Only believers are gifted spiritually. . . .Talents depend on natural power, gifts on spiritual endowment (Leslie B. Flynn, *19 Gifts of the Spirit*).

C. View #3 - A Middle Way which suggests that spiritual gifts can be either the energizing of God-given natural talents or the creation of entirely new talents.

Areas of Disagreement among Christians Concerning Spiritual Gifts (continued)

1. Note that logically, at least, it is not necessary for these two views to be mutually exclusive. It is at least possible that both types of spiritual gifts exist, some that are latent and some that are new.

2. Perhaps a more useful way to think about this would be to remember that gifts are the "manifestation" of the Spirit for the common good.

3. The Spirit being manifested is the emphasis not the means by which it happens. It is always a "gracious gift" when this happens. It always happens solely because of the Spirit's decision and because of the Spirit's power. Thus, whether the Spirit chooses to empower a natural capacity or create an entirely new one, each is a "charisma" — a gift of grace. A God given ability to teach exercised by a non-believer is a gracious gift (given by the Spirit in creation) but it is not a "manifestation of the Spirit" until that person submits themselves to the Holy Spirit and uses that gift under his direction and for his purposes.

II. Are All the Gifts Listed in the New Testament Available Today?

A. Some traditions answer "No."

1. Some traditions argue for the ceasing of certain gifts: usually apostleship, prophecy, tongues and interpretation (sometimes miracles).

2. There are at least two theological reasons why this is believed.

   a. First, there is a concern for safeguarding God's revelation in Scripture.

   If apostles, prophets, and tongues continue to function as a means of ongoing revelation, the integrity of Scripture is potentially put at risk. Again and again in the history of the Church, people have come along that claimed a new, prophetic revelation which contradicted or went beyond the claims of Scripture. The scriptural testimony to Jesus as God's final Word cannot be compromised and these theological traditions do not see a way to reconcile the possibility of new revelations with that fact.

b. Second, the role of the apostles as the "foundation" of the Church seems to imply a unique place in Church history.

The Gospels and the Book of Acts are seen as a pivot point of history during which God works uniquely and unrepeatably to change his revelation from the Old Covenant to the New Covenant. This is accomplished by the granting of new revelations (which form the New Testament Scriptures) and signs and wonders which confirm and establish this testimony as authentic. The Church now is to exist by the testimony of that Word, guarding the deposit of faith but not adding to it or subtracting from it.

(1) Jude 1.3 (ESV) - Beloved, although I was very eager to write to you about our common salvation, I found it necessary to write appealing to you to contend for the faith that was once for all delivered to the saints.

(2) Heb. 1.1-3 (ESV) - Long ago, at many times and in many ways, God spoke to our fathers by the prophets, [2] but in these last days he has spoken to us by his Son, whom he appointed the heir of all things, through whom also he created the world. [3] He is the radiance of the glory of God and the exact imprint of his nature, and he upholds the universe by the word of his power. After making purification for sins, he sat down at the right hand of the Majesty on high.

(3) Gal. 1.8-9 (ESV) - But even if we or an angel from heaven should preach to you a gospel contrary to the one we preached to you, let him be accursed. [9] As we have said before, so now I say again: If anyone is preaching to you a gospel contrary to the one you received, let him be accursed.

B. Some traditions answer "Yes."

"All may agree that there appears no new revelation to be expected concerning God in Christ. But there appears to be no good reason why the living God, who both speaks and acts (in contrast to dead idols), cannot use the gift of prophecy to give particular local guidance to a church, nation or individual, or to warn or encourage by way of prediction as well as by reminders, in full accord with the written word of Scripture, by which all such utterances must be tested. Certainly the NT does not see it as the job of the prophet to be a doctrinal innovator, but to deliver the word the Spirit gives him in line with the truth once for all delivered to the saints (Jude 3), to challenge and encourage our faith" (J. P. Baker, "Prophecy," *New Bible Dictionary*, 2nd Edition, J. D. Douglas and others, eds.).

1. The ministry of Jesus and the example of the Apostles and the New Testament Church is our inspired model for ministry and all of them used miraculous gifts in ministry.

2. The only time that Scripture speaks to the question of when gifts will cease it refers to the return of Christ (1 Cor. 13.8-12).

3. The Holy Spirit is free and sovereign. He can give (or withhold) any gift at any time for whatever purpose he chooses (1 Cor. 12.11 – gives as he determines).

4. The Craig S. Keener reading (*Gift and Giver*—pp. 89-112) makes the basic arguments for the view that all are available.

APPENDIX 20
The Role of the Holy Spirit in Spiritual Guidance
Terry G. Cornett

Through the Holy Spirit, God has made himself available to believers so that they can be in constant, friendship relationship with him, receiving ongoing guidance and direction as to what he wants from them.

I. Key Texts

A. Rom. 8.14 (ESV) - For all who are led by the Spirit of God are sons of God.

B. Isa. 63.10-14 (ESV) - But they rebelled and grieved his Holy Spirit; therefore he turned to be their enemy, and himself fought against them. [11] Then he remembered the days of old, of Moses and his people. Where is he who brought them up out of the sea with the shepherds of his flock? Where is he who put in the midst of them his Holy Spirit, [12] who caused his glorious arm to go at the right hand of Moses, who divided the waters before them to make for himself an everlasting name, [13] who led them through the depths? Like a horse in the desert, they did not stumble. [14] Like livestock that go down into the valley, the Spirit of the Lord gave them rest. So you led your people, to make for yourself a glorious name.

C. John 10.1-5 (ESV) - Truly, truly, I say to you, he who does not enter the sheepfold by the door but climbs in by another way, that man is a thief and a robber. [2] But he who enters by the door is the shepherd of the sheep. [3] To him the gatekeeper opens. The sheep hear his voice, and he calls his own sheep by name and leads them out. [4] When he has brought out all his own, he goes before them, and the sheep follow him, for they know his voice. [5] A stranger they will not follow, but they will flee from him, for they do not know the voice of strangers.

D. John 14.25-26 (ESV) - These things I have spoken to you while I am still with you. [26] But the Helper, the Holy Spirit, whom the Father will send in my name, he will teach you all things and bring to your remembrance all that I have said to you.

E. John 16.13 (ESV) - When the Spirit of truth comes, he will guide you into all the truth, for he will not speak on his own authority, but whatever he hears he will speak, and he will declare to you the things that are to come.

F. Acts 16.7-8 (ESV) - And when they had come up to Mysia, they attempted to go into Bithynia, but the Spirit of Jesus did not allow them. [8] So, passing by Mysia, they went down to Troas (cf. Acts 20.22-23).

II. Why is the Guidance of the Holy Spirit so important?

Christian, then, recognizes that when faced with the alternatives of good and evil, there is no choice; one must do good. But the greater challenge comes when we are faced with multiple alternatives that are all morally good. The question then becomes, which is the good to which God is calling me? And the good then becomes the enemy of the best, since it is quite possible for us to fill our days doing good things but neglecting the one thing that we must do and to which we are called. . . .Every choice is then both a yes and a no. . .If I take on this assignment or this job, it means saying no to other opportunities. If I choose to spend my day in this way, it means I am saying no to other activities that might have filled my day. And surely this is what makes decisions making a challenge: we cannot be everywhere and we cannot do everything. There are many good things that we might do, and we cannot do them all. Again, this would be a terrifying and impossible burden were it not for the providential care of God. He is a God who is present and alive in all that is—the land, the sea, and the sky—but also a God who is personally present in each one of us. We are not alone! This is exceedingly good news. . . .When we make a choice, the Spirit is with us. Indeed we speak of God as Shepherd, that is, as one who guides (Ps. 23). And we experience this guidance most keenly in our times of choosing. Still, our decision making is our responsibility; it is our act of choosing in response to the options, problems, and opportunities that are placed before us. God does not choose for us, and

The Role of the Holy Spirit in Spiritual Guidance (continued)

we cannot expect others to make our choices for us, not if we want to accept adult responsibility for our lives. Indeed the capacity to discern well and make wise decisions is a critical sign of spiritual maturity. And further, it is something that we learn as we mature in faith and grow in wisdom.

~ Gordon T. Smith.

The Voice of Jesus: Discernment, Prayer, and the Witness of the Spirit. pp 130-132.

III. How Do We Hear God's Voice?

A. Know what God the Spirit has already spoken: God's Written Word

1. The Scriptures are the record of the Spirit's guidance. The Scriptures are not only the infallible judge of guidance or prophecy, they are also our training in the recognition of God's voice.

2. John 5.46-47 (ESV) - If you believed Moses, you would believe me; for he wrote of me. [47] But if you do not believe his writings, how will you believe my words?

B. Set your heart to obey

1. Usually, the problem is NOT with our hearing!

   a. Ps. 119.10 (ESV) - With my whole heart I seek you; let me not wander from your commandments!

   b. The fundamental question relating to guidance is not whether I will be able to hear God speak but whether I intend to obey what he says.

2. God is a competent, clear-speaking guide.

    a. John 10.2-5, 27 (ESV) - But he who enters by the door is the shepherd of the sheep. [3] To him the gatekeeper opens. The sheep hear his voice, and he calls his own sheep by name and leads them out. [4] When he has brought out all his own, he goes before them, and the sheep follow him, for they know his voice. [5] A stranger they will not follow, but they will flee from him, for they do not know the voice of strangers. . . . [27] My sheep hear my voice, and I know them, and they follow me.

    b. The metaphors of Scripture describe a God who will be heard!

        (1) The images given by God to describe his leadership are very helpful. God is a king, a parent, a shepherd. The biblical question is seldom, "How do we hear?" Jesus says quite confidently that his sheep know his voice. Like all kings or parents or shepherds, God has no difficulty communicating to us in ways that we will understand.

        (2) How many of us, for example, find that the IRS has difficulty communicating with us that we need to pay taxes? How many of us just forget about April 15th and never think about it again once it is passed?

        (3) How many of you as kids sat around and agonized whether you were going to be able to recognize your parent's voice. What initiative did you take as a child to make sure you could hear and understand your parents?

        (4) In the same manner, God takes the initiative to communicate his will to his people.

The Role of the Holy Spirit in Spiritual Guidance (continued)

 c. If God is silent it usually means that we are either free to choose among the good choices he has placed at our disposal, or alternatively, that we are operating under a preexisting command.

  (1) If God wants us to do something, he will make it clear to the listening heart.

  (2) When God has a already communicated his will through the Scriptures, the question will not be hearing but obeying.

 d. The importance of a listening heart.

  The foundational ground rule: We cannot be ignoring God or running away from obedience and then claim that God is not saying anything.

  (1) God's Church as the natural environment for listening.

   (a) The family analogy holds true. My children came home after school everyday, ate at my table, lived in my house, and participated in our family life. Because that was true, they could be confident that they were hearing what I wanted from them. We must do the same in our spiritual walk.

   (b) If we ignore our relationship with the family of God and do not spend time in his presence, and hearing his Word, he will speak, but we will likely not attend to his voice. On the other hand, active participation in family life is an important part of listening

   (c) In my own experience God often speaks to me at church. Sometimes through the sermon and sometimes along a line completely different from the sermon or worship emphasis. The point is that I am at his family table. He can speak through the preacher or he can simply capture my attention and speak directly to my heart but I must participate in the family to have a reasonable expectation of receiving direction. If we run away from time with God's family (like the prodigal son) we cannot, then, claim the excuse that we do not hear him saying anything.

(d) Hearing the voice of God is not a private function. It takes place in community. We hear the voice of God best when we listen along with others.

(e) Our pastors and spiritual leaders have a unique role to play in this process.

(f) Heb. 13.17 (ESV) - Obey your leaders and submit to them, for they are keeping watch over your souls, as those who will have to give an account. Let them do this with joy and not with groaning, for that would be of no advantage to you.

(g) Consulting our pastoral leadership for their insights and counsel is a natural starting point for decisions where God's will is not clear.

(h) Our brothers and sisters in Christ are also a rich resource for speaking the mind of Christ to us.

(i) 1 Cor. 12.7 (ESV) - To each is given the manifestation of the Spirit for the common good.

(j) 1 Cor. 14.26 (ESV) - What then, brothers? When you come together, each one has a hymn, a lesson, a revelation, a tongue, or an interpretation. Let all things be done for building up.

(k) Prov. 27.17 (ESV) - Iron sharpens iron, and one man sharpens another.

(l) Prov. 11.14 (ESV) - Where there is no guidance, a people falls, but in an abundance of counselors there is safety.

(m) Listening to the voice of the Spirit necessarily means that we must listen to the counsel of the church community and its leaders.

The Role of the Holy Spirit in Spiritual Guidance (continued)

    (2)   The role of attention.

> *I make it my business to persevere in his Holy presence, wherein I keep myself by a simple attention and a general fond regard to God, which I may call an ACTUAL PRESENCE of God; or, to speak better, an habitual, silent, and secret conversation of the soul with God, which often causes me joys and raptures inwardly, and sometimes also outwardly, so great that I am forced to use means to moderate them and prevent their appearance to others.*

> ~ Brother Lawrence quoted in Dallas Willard. **Hearing God.**

    (3)   A Prayer from Saint Anselm of Canterbury (1033-1109).

Teach me to seek you

And as I seek you, show yourself to me,

For I cannot seek you unless you show me how,

And I will never find you unless you show yourself to me.

Let me seek you by desiring you,

And desire you by seeking you;

Let me find you by loving you,

And love you in finding you.

Amen.

IV. For further reading:

Richard J. Foster. Chapter 12. "Guidance." *Celebration of Discipline: The Path to Spiritual Growth.* San Francisco: HarperSanFrancisco, 1998.

Gordon T. Smith. *The Voice of Jesus: Discernment, Prayer and the Witness of the Spirit.* Downers Grove, IL: InterVarsity Press, 2003

Charles Stanley. *How to Listen to God.* Nashville: Thomas Nelson, 1985.

Mark Water. *Knowing God's Will Made Easier.* Peabody, MA: Hendrickson, 1998.

APPENDIX 21

Some of the Ways in Which Christians Disagree about Sanctification

Rev. Terry G. Cornett

I. Two Key Questions

A. The First Question: *Can a person be entirely sanctified (completely free from sin), in this present life?*

1. Reformed/Baptistic and some Pentecostal theologies say NO.

2. Holiness and some Pentecostal theologies say YES.

B. The Second Question: *Does the experience of sanctification include a second distinct experience with God, received by grace through faith?*

What you believe about the first question, tends to influence what you believe about the second.

1. If you believe that complete holiness must wait for the transforming event of death or Christ's return, you hope to grow in holiness but there is no distinct point in this life where it can be achieved.

2. If you believe that complete holiness is attainable, you know it must come through a transforming event (you can't work your way into holiness). So holiness and Pentecostal-holiness groups say there is a distinct second experience.

II. Traditional Reformation Teaching

A. Sanctification is begun at salvation and continues progressively until glorification. God completely sanctifies us positionally at the moment of salvation, but practical sanctification is worked out in our experience gradually and daily.

B. Sin is primarily defined as "falling short of God's glory."

C. Arguments in favor:

1. Jesus taught us to pray daily, "Forgive us our trespasses" (Matt. 6.12) and added "But if you do not forgive others their trespasses, neither will your Father forgive your trespasses" (Matt. 6.15).

2. The Corinthian church was identified by Paul as "sanctified by Christ Jesus and called to be holy" but in practice was anything but. Paul had to say in 1 Corinthians 3.3, "For you are still of the flesh. For while there is jealousy and strife among you, are you not of the flesh and behaving only in a human way?" Paul understood the difference between being sanctified in God's sight but not yet sanctified in practice.

    a. Experience teaches us that:

    (1) We sin.

    (2) People who claim perfection tend to become legalistic, condemning, boastful, and tend to deny sin when it occurs.

Some of the Ways in Which Christians Disagree about Sanctification (continued)

b. Romans 7 – This passage is understood as describing Paul's experience following conversion.

c. Complete sinless perfection is not attainable in this life. When the word "Perfect" occurs in Scripture it is understood as "complete" or "mature." *Glorification is when sinlessness is achieved.* Sanctification is the movement toward holiness that draws on the resources given at salvation.

d. Most important historical proponent: Martin Luther

Luther spoke about Christians as *"simul justus et peccator"*- at one and the same time a righteous man and a sinner. He believed that this paradox will not find resolution until faith become sight. Lutheranism in no way condones sin. Rather it recognizes "that where sin abounded, grace did much more abound."

III. Holiness Movements

A. Sanctification is a second and distinct experience from salvation. Like salvation it is received by grace through faith and is frequently spoken of as "the Baptism in the Holy Spirit."

Entire Sanctification more commonly designated as "sanctification," "holiness," "Christian perfection," or "perfect love," represents that second definite stage in Christian experience wherein, by the baptism with the Holy Spirit, administered by Jesus Christ, and received instantaneously by faith, the justified believer is delivered from inbred sin, and consequently is saved from all unholy tempers, cleansed from all moral defilement, made perfect in love and introduced into full and abiding fellowship with God.

~ Doctrinal Statement of The First General Holiness Assembly held in Chicago, May, 1885
[Robert M. Anderson, **Vision of the Disinherited**]

Some of the Ways in Which Christians Disagree about Sanctification (continued)

B. Sin is primarily defined as "knowing, willful disobedience."

1. The concept of Christian Perfection [entire sanctification] is carefully defined.

    Perfection is not: perfect knowledge (ignorance remains), not freedom from mistakes, not free from weakness or character flaws, not free from temptation, not free from the need to grow, [See John Wesley, *On Christian Perfection*] It is not, a loss of the ability to sin. There is no point, short of glorification, where people could not fall.

    Perfection is: Walking in love by faith so that one does not sin willfully and habitually.

2. There is still a process of sanctification that follows the event of sanctification.

    I believe this perfection is always wrought in the soul by a simple act of faith; consequently in an instant. But I believe [in] a gradual work, both preceding and following that instant. As to the time, I believe this instant generally is the instant of death, the moment before the soul leaves the body. But I believe it may be ten, twenty, or forty years before. I believe it is usually many years after justification.

    ~ Brief Thoughts on Christian Perfection.
    The Works of John Wesley. Vol. 11, p. 466.

    Some holiness groups disagree with Wesley about timing. They believe entire sanctification can, and should, come more quickly.

Some of the Ways in Which Christians Disagree about Sanctification (continued)

C. Arguments for:

1. It is commanded by Jesus and the Apostles

    Matt. 5.48 - "Therefore you are to be perfect, as your heavenly Father is perfect." Compare with Apostle's injunction (1 John 5.3 - This is love for God: to obey his commands. And his commands are not burdensome).

2. It is the logical implication of what happens when an all-powerful God sets his Spirit to work against sin in our lives.

3. It seems to be frequently assumed by Scripture to be what happens in the life of the believer.

4. Romans 7 – This passage is understood as describing Paul's experience before conversion.

D. Most important historical proponent: John Wesley (who learned from the Puritan writer William Law)

E. Key Document: "A Plain Account of Christian Perfection."

    Wesley's key concern was to avoid conceding the possibility of perfection because he felt it impugned God's nature and power. (Don't say that God cannot or will not do what he clearly desires). It is an issue of faith for Wesley. Even if he had never seen this happen he would still believe in God's ability to accomplish his desire for our holiness.

Some of the Ways in Which Christians Disagree about Sanctification (continued)

IV. Putting it Together: Theological Common Ground and Key Implications

What Reformed and Holiness Christians agree on:

A. Sanctification is becoming like Christ and is the aim of the Christian life. [Scripture teaches us that this [holiness] is the goal of our calling- John Calvin, "Institutes of the Christian Religion].

B. Sanctification begins at the moment of salvation and faith is its sole condition (Doctrinal Minutes of the Methodist Conferences 1744-47).

C. Sanctification is both imputed and imparted and comes only by the grace of God.

D. Sanctification involves both a unique point of decision[1] and an on-going process of living out that decision.

[1] *For Reformed theology this point is conversion, for Holiness theologies it is conversion and a second experience of grace with the Holy Spirit.*

Denominational Statements on "Sanctification"

Statements from
Lutheran, Reformed,
and Baptist
Denominations

Church of the Lutheran Brethren
http://www.clba.org/aboutus.phtml

Sanctification

Sanctification is God's gracious, continual work of spiritual renewal and growth in the life of every justified person. Through the means of grace, the Holy Spirit works to reproduce the character of Christ within the lives of all believers, instructing and urging them to live out their new nature. The Holy Spirit enables believers more and more to resist the devil, to overcome the world, and to count themselves dead to sin but alive to God in Christ Jesus. The Holy Spirit produces spiritual fruit in and bestows spiritual gifts upon all believers. He calls, empowers and equips them to serve God in the home, in the community, and as part of the Church Universal. The process of sanctification will be complete only when the believer reaches glory.

Presbyterian Church in America
http://www.pcanet.org/general/cof_chapxi-xv.htm#chapxiii

The Westminster Confession of Faith

CHAP. XIII. - Of Sanctification.

1. They, who are once effectually called, and regenerated, having a new heart, and a new spirit created in them, are further sanctified, really and personally, through the virtue of Christ's death and resurrection, by His Word and Spirit dwelling in them, the dominion of the whole body of sin is destroyed, and the several lusts thereof are more and more weakened and mortified; and they more and more quickened and strengthened in all saving graces, to the practice of true holiness, without which no man shall see the Lord.

2. This sanctification is throughout, in the whole man; yet imperfect in this life, there abiding still some remnants of corruption in every part; whence ariseth a continual and irreconcilable war, the flesh lusting against the Spirit, and the Spirit against the flesh.

Denominational Statements on "Sanctification" (continued)

3. In which war, although the remaining corruption, for a time, may much prevail; yet, through the continual supply of strength from the sanctifying Spirit of Christ, the regenerate part doth overcome; and so, the saints grow in grace, perfecting holiness in the fear of God.

Southern Baptist Convention

http://www.sbc.net/bfm/bfm2000.asp#iv

Salvation involves the redemption of the whole man, and is offered freely to all who accept Jesus Christ as Lord and Saviour, who by His own blood obtained eternal redemption for the believer. In its broadest sense salvation includes regeneration, justification, sanctification, and glorification. There is no salvation apart from personal faith in Jesus Christ as Lord.

1. Regeneration, or the new birth, is a work of God's grace whereby believers become new creatures in Christ Jesus. It is a change of heart wrought by the Holy Spirit through conviction of sin, to which the sinner responds in repentance toward God and faith in the Lord Jesus Christ. Repentance and faith are inseparable experiences of grace.

   Repentance is a genuine turning from sin toward God. Faith is the acceptance of Jesus Christ and commitment of the entire personality to Him as Lord and Saviour.

2. Justification is God's gracious and full acquittal upon principles of His righteousness of all sinners who repent and believe in Christ. Justification brings the believer unto a relationship of peace and favor with God.

3. Sanctification is the experience, beginning in regeneration, by which the believer is set apart to God's purposes, and is enabled to progress toward moral and spiritual maturity through the presence and power of the Holy Spirit dwelling in him. Growth in grace should continue throughout the regenerate person's life.

4. Glorification is the culmination of salvation and is the final blessed and abiding state of the redeemed.

   Gen. 3.15; Exod. 3.14-17; 6.2-8; Matt. 1.21; 4.17; 16.21-26; 27.22-28.6; Luke 1.68-69; 2.28-32; John 1.11-14,29; 3.3-21,36; 5.24; 10.9,28-29; 15.1-16; 17.17; Acts

2.21; 4.12; 15.11; 16.30-31; 17.30-31; 20.32; Rom. 1.16-18; 2.4; 3.23-25; 4.3ff.; 5.8-10; 6.1-23; 8.1-18,29-39; 10.9-10,13; 13.11-14; 1 Cor. 1.18,30; 6.19-20; 15.10; 2 Cor. 5.17-20; Gal. 2.20; 3.13; 5.22-25; 6.15; Eph. 1.7; 2.8-22; 4.11-16; Phil. 2.12-13; Col. 1.9-22; 3.1ff.; 1 Thess. 5.23-24; 2 Tim. 1.12; Titus 2.11-14; Heb. 2.1-3; 5.8-9; 9.24-28; 11.1-12.8,14; James 2.14-26; 1 Pet. 1.2-23; 1 John 1.6-2.11; Rev. 3.20; 21.1-22.5.

Statements from Holiness Denominations

Church of the Nazarene

www.nazarene.org/gensec/we_believe.html

Articles of Faith

We believe that entire sanctification is that act of God, subsequent to regeneration, by which believers are made free from original sin, or depravity, and brought into a state of entire devotement to God, and the holy obedience of love made perfect. It is wrought by the baptism with the Holy Spirit, and comprehends in one experience the cleansing of the heart from sin and the abiding, indwelling presence of the Holy Spirit, empowering the believer for life and service. Entire sanctification is provided by the blood of Jesus, is wrought instantaneously by faith, preceded by entire consecration; and to this work and state of grace the Holy Spirit bears witness. This experience is also known by various terms representing its different phases, such as "Christian perfection," "perfect love," "heart purity," "the baptism with the Holy Spirit," "the fullness of the blessing," and "Christian holiness."

We believe that there is a marked distinction between a pure heart and a mature character. The former is obtained in an instant, the result of entire sanctification; the latter is the result of growth in grace. We believe that the grace of entire sanctification includes the impulse to grow in grace. However, this impulse must be consciously nurtured, and careful attention given to the requisites and processes of spiritual development and improvement in Christlikeness of character and personality. Without such purposeful endeavor one's witness may be impaired and the grace itself frustrated and ultimately lost.

(Jer. 31.31-34; Ezek. 36.25-27; Mal. 3.2-3; Matt. 3.11-12; Luke 3.16-17; John 7.37-39; 14.15-23; 17.6-20; Acts 1.5; 2.1-4; 15.8-9; Rom. 6.11-13, 19; 8.1-4, 8-14; 12.1-2; 2 Cor. 6.14-7.1; Gal. 2.20; 5.16-25; Eph. 3.14-21; 5.17-18, 25-27; Phil. 3.10-15; Col. 3.1-17; 1 Thess. 5.23-24; Heb. 4.9-11; 10.10-17; 12.1-2; 13.12; 1 John 1.7, 9) ("Christian perfection," "perfect love": Deut. 30.6; Matt. 5.43-48; 22.37-40; Rom. 12.9-21;

13.8-10; 1 Cor. 13; Phil. 3.10-15; Heb. 6.1; 1 John 4.17-18 "Heart purity": Matt. 5.8; Acts 15.8-9; 1 Pet. 1.22; 1 John 3.3 "Baptism with the Holy Spirit": Jer. 31.31-34; Ezek. 36.25-27; Mal. 3.2-3; Matt. 3.11-12; Luke 3.16-17; Acts 1.5; 2.1-4; 15.8-9 "Fullness of the blessing": Rom. 15.29 "Christian holiness": Matt. 5.1-7.29; John 15.1-11; Rom. 12.1-15.3; 2 Cor. 7.1; Eph. 4.17-5.20; Phil. 1.9-11; 3.12-15; Col. 2.20-3.17; 1 Thess. 3.13;.7-8;5.23; 2 Tim. 2.19-22; Heb. 10.19-25; 12.14; 13.20-21; 1 Pet. 1.15-16; 2 Pet. 1.1-11; 3.18; Jude 20-21)

Free Methodist Church

www.fmc-canada.org/articles.htm

Articles of Religion

Entire sanctification is that work of the Holy Spirit, subsequent to regeneration, by which the fully consecrated believer, upon exercise of faith in the atoning blood of Christ, is cleansed in that moment from all inward sin and empowered for service. The resulting relationship is attested by the witness of the Holy Spirit and is maintained by faith and obedience. Entire sanctification enables the believer to love God with all his heart, soul, strength, and mind, and his neighbor as himself, and it prepares him for greater growth in grace. (Lev. 20.7-8; John 14.16-17; 17.19; Acts 1.8; 2.4; 15.8-9; Rom. 5.3-5; 8.12-17; 12.1-2; 1 Cor 6.11; 12.4-11; Gal. 5.22-25; Eph. 4.22-24; 1 Thess 4.7; 5.23-24; 2 Thess 2.13; Heb. 10.14)

Wesleyan Church

www.wesleyan.org/doctrine.htm

The Articles of Religion

We believe that sanctification is that work of the Holy Spirit by which the child of God is separated from sin unto God and is enabled to love God with all the heart and to walk in all His holy commandments blameless. Sanctification is initiated at the moment of justification and regeneration. From that moment there is a gradual or progressive sanctification as the believer walks with God and daily grows in grace and in a more perfect obedience to God. This prepares for the crisis of entire sanctification which is wrought instantaneously when believers present themselves as living sacrifices, holy and acceptable to God, through faith in Jesus Christ, being effected by the baptism with the Holy Spirit who cleanses the heart from all inbred sin. The crisis of entire sanctification perfects the believer in love and empowers that person for effective service. It is followed by lifelong growth in grace and the knowledge of our Lord and Savior Jesus Christ. The life of holiness continues through faith in the sanctifying blood of Christ and evidences itself by loving obedience to God's revealed will.

Gen. 17.1; Deut. 30.6; Ps. 130.8; Isa. 6.1-6; Ezek. 36.25-29; Matt. 5.8, 48; Luke 1.74-75; 3.16-17; 24.49; John 17.1-26; Acts 1.4-5, 8; 2.1-4; 15.8-9; 26.18; Rom. 8.3-4; 1 Cor. 1.2; 6.11; 2 Cor. 7.1; Eph. 4.13, 24; 5.25-27; 1 Thess. 3.10, 12-13; 4.3, 7-8; 5.23-24; 2 Thess. 2.13; Titus 2.11-14; Heb. 10.14; 12.14; 13.12; James 3.17-18; 4.8; 1 Peter 1.2; 2 Peter 1.4; 1 John 1.7, 9; 3.8-9; 4.17-18; Jude 24.

APPENDIX 23

Documenting Your Work
A Guide to Help You Give Credit Where Credit Is Due
The Urban Ministry Institute

Plagiarism is using another person's ideas as if they belonged to you without giving them proper credit. In academic work it is just as wrong to steal a person's ideas as it is to steal a person's property. These ideas may come from the author of a book, an article you have read, or from a fellow student. The way to avoid plagiarism is to carefully use "notes" (textnotes, footnotes, endnotes, etc.) and a "Works Cited" section to help people who read your work know when an idea is one you thought of, and when you are borrowing an idea from another person.

Avoiding Plagiarism

A citation reference is required in a paper whenever you use ideas or information that came from another person's work.

Using Citation References

All citation references involve two parts:

- Notes in the body of your paper placed next to each quotation which came from an outside source.

- A "Works Cited" page at the end of your paper or project which gives information about the sources you have used

There are three basic kinds of notes: parenthetical notes, footnotes, and endnotes. At The Urban Ministry Institute, we recommend that students use parenthetical notes. These notes give the author's last name(s), the date the book was published, and the page number(s) on which you found the information. Example:

Using Notes in Your Paper

> In trying to understand the meaning of Genesis 14.1-24, it is important to recognize that in biblical stories "the place where dialogue is first introduced will be an important moment in revealing the character of the speaker . . ." (Kaiser and Silva 1994, 73). This is certainly true of the character of Melchizedek who speaks words of blessing. This identification of Melchizedek as a positive spiritual influence is reinforced by the fact that he is the King of Salem, since Salem means "safe, at peace" (Wiseman 1996, 1045).

Creating a Works Cited Page

A "Works Cited" page should be placed at the end of your paper. This page:

- lists every source you quoted in your paper

- is in alphabetical order by author's last name

- includes the date of publication and information about the publisher

The following formatting rules should be followed:

1. Title

The title "Works Cited" should be used and centered on the first line of the page following the top margin.

2. Content

Each reference should list:

- the author's full name (last name first)

- the date of publication

- the title and any special information (Revised edition, 2nd edition, reprint) taken from the cover or title page should be noted

- the city where the publisher is headquartered followed by a colon and the name of the publisher

3. Basic form

- Each piece of information should be separated by a period.

- The second line of a reference (and all following lines) should be indented.

- Book titles should be underlined (or italicized).

- Article titles should be placed in quotes.

Example:

Fee, Gordon D. 1991. *Gospel and Spirit: Issues in New Testament Hermeneutics.* Peabody, MA: Hendrickson Publishers.

Documenting Your Work (continued)

4. Special Forms

A book with multiple authors:

> Kaiser, Walter C., and Moisés Silva. 1994. *An Introduction to Biblical Hermeneutics: The Search for Meaning.* Grand Rapids: Zondervan Publishing House.

An edited book:

> Greenway, Roger S., ed. 1992. *Discipling the City: A Comprehensive Approach to Urban Mission.* 2nd ed. Grand Rapids: Baker Book House.

A book that is part of a series:

> Morris, Leon. 1971. *The Gospel According to John.* Grand Rapids: Wm. B. Eerdmans Publishing Co. The New International Commentary on the New Testament. Gen. ed. F. F. Bruce.

An article in a reference book:

> Wiseman, D. J. "Salem." 1982. In *New Bible Dictionary.* Leicester, England - Downers Grove, IL: InterVarsity Press. Eds. I. H. Marshall and others.

(An example of a "Works Cited" page is located on the next page.)

(An example of a "Works Cited" page is located on the next page.)

Standard guides to documenting academic work in the areas of philosophy, religion, theology, and ethics include:

> Atchert, Walter S., and Joseph Gibaldi. 1985. *The MLA Style Manual.* New York: Modern Language Association.

> *The Chicago Manual of Style.* 1993. 14th ed. Chicago: The University of Chicago Press.

> Turabian, Kate L. 1987. *A Manual for Writers of Term Papers, Theses, and Dissertations.* 5th edition. Bonnie Bertwistle Honigsblum, ed. Chicago: The University of Chicago Press.

For Further Research

Works Cited

Fee, Gordon D. 1991. *Gospel and Spirit: Issues in New Testament Hermeneutics*. Peabody, MA: Hendrickson Publishers.

Greenway, Roger S., ed. 1992. *Discipling the City: A Comprehensive Approach to Urban Mission*. 2nd ed. Grand Rapids: Baker Book House.

Kaiser, Walter C., and Moisés Silva. 1994. *An Introduction to Biblical Hermeneutics: The Search for Meaning*. Grand Rapids: Zondervan Publishing House.

Morris, Leon. 1971. *The Gospel According to John*. Grand Rapids: Wm. B. Eerdmans Publishing Co. *The New International Commentary on the New Testament*. Gen. ed. F. F. Bruce.

Wiseman, D. J. "Salem." 1982. In *New Bible Dictionary*. Leicester, England-Downers Grove, IL: InterVarsity Press. Eds. I. H. Marshall and others.

Made in the USA
Coppell, TX
05 January 2025